ALWAYS ON THE RUN

ALWAYS ON THE RUN

By Larry Csonka and Jim Kiick

with Dave Anderson

RANDOM HOUSE NEW YORK

Library of Congress Cataloging in Publication Data

Csonka, Larry.
Always on the run.

SUMMARY: Two stars of the Miami Dolphins exchange their thoughts
about their lives, football, Coach Shula, and other topics.

1. Csonka, Larry. 2. Kiick, Jim. 3. Miami Dolphins (Football club). 4.
Backfield play (Football)
[1. Csonka, Larry. 2. Kiick, Jim. 3. Miami Dolphins (Football club). 4.
Football] I. Kiick, Jim.
II. Anderson, Dave. III. Title.
GV939.A1C78   796.33'2'0922   73-5052
ISBN 0-394-48589-9

Manufactured in the United States of America
First Edition

To every guy who enjoys having a beer with his shirttail out when he's watching us on TV . . .

. . . and to every kid who ever had goose pimples when somebody was chasing him

Contents

Introduction

When we were working on the book, I was with Larry Csonka one evening as he entered the Country Club of Miami to meet some friends. Recognizing him, a middle-aged lady stared at him for a moment, then said:

"I know you . . . you're Larry Csonka . . . no, Jim Kiick."

"I'm one of 'em," he replied, smiling. "I'm Zonk."

As football players, they almost are interchangeable. Each is a running back for the Miami Dolphins, the NFL champions, unbeaten through Super Bowl VII last season for an unprecedented 17–0 won-lost record.

"Zonk attacks the earth," says Bob Griese, their quarterback.

"Jim is the complete athlete," says Don Shula, their coach.

But as men, each is so different. Zonk grew up on a farm in Stow, Ohio, near Akron, while Jim grew up on a street corner in Lincoln Park, New Jersey, near New York City. Zonk is a gregarious storyteller; Jim is a subtle listener.

But each has a flair befitting his status as a celebrity in the Miami area. Zonk owns a Bentley and Jim cruises around in a silver Mark IV, both advertised as rare and exclusive models. Except that in Miami they're not that exclusive. As we drove along one day, I heard Jim grumble: "That's the third one I've seen in the last twenty minutes."

Until we began our tape-recorded conversations, I had known them only as football players, not as people. As a sports columnist for *The New York Times* with a preference for pro football, I had often seen them play. After the games, I had listened to them and questioned them. One time Zonk and a defensive end, Jim Riley, were sitting nude on a table in the dressing room. Riley was gulping a Coke when, suddenly, it spilled. As the cold liquid splashed his skin, Riley jumped away. Soon it oozed against Zonk's bare butt. He didn't move. He sighed and shook his head slowly, but he never moved.

I don't remember any of the questions and answers that day, but I remember that Zonk never moved.

Apparently he was simply too tired, because under normal conditions he reacts emotionally. Usually our conversations took place in motel rooms—theirs on Dolphin trips, mine in Miami—and almost always a small crisis interrupted us. Once, high in the Essex House in New York, their TV set wasn't working properly. It was supposed to provide a movie on a closed-circuit channel. When the movie did not appear after several phone calls to the desk clerk, Zonk began to shake the set. The room began to shake, too.

"I ought to throw this thing out the window into the street," he grumbled. "If more people did that, they'd make sure all the TV sets worked like they should."

At the Edgewater Hyatt House in Long Beach, California, before the Super Bowl game, a room-service waiter arrived an hour after Zonk had ordered. The waiter had six glasses of Coke, each packed with ice.

"I ordered six bottles of Coke," he said. "Not six *glasses* with Coke in them. I'm not paying for them. Take them back."

Through each crisis, Jim never stirred from the bed he was sprawled on. Maybe he was saving himself for a crisis during a game. In the Dolphins' three post-season games, he scored a total of four touchdowns, including the decisive touchdown in each game.

You'll read of Jim's "bad attitude." But no coach ever complained about his attitude near the goal line.

His attitude toward working on the book was enthusiastic, too, as was Zonk's. The day I presented them with the completed manuscript for their approval, Jim sat on a couch, read it quickly, changed a few words, finished, strolled into the backyard and sunned himself. Zonk, meanwhile, sat at a dining-room table, making thoughtful changes, suggesting slight revisions.

"Fullbacks really are slower than halfbacks," I said, winking.

"No," said Zonk slowly, "Jim just meant it the first time."

DAVE ANDERSON

ALWAYS ON THE RUN

1

Who Are These Guys?

I'm Larry Csonka, in the straight-up type.

I'm Jim Kiick, in the slanty type.

That's perfect for Jim, because he is the slanty type. His eyes are always half closed, like he's asleep. And he doesn't always believe what I tell him. Like when I was a kid on the farm in Stow, Ohio, my dad grew tomatoes that belonged at the State Fair, that's how big they were. I loved those tomatoes. We even had a border collie that loved tomatoes. One time I was eating a tomato from one side when that dog came up and took a bite out of the other side without touching me. That's how big that tomato was.

Get the hat.

Whenever one of us says "Get the hat," it means cut the bullshit. But that's true about the tomato. It really was that big. But ol' Kiicker just can't understand that because he grew up in Lincoln Park, New Jersey, not far from New York City. He's really a hood.

We've got big tomatoes in Jersey, but I never saw a dog eat any tomatoes.

It might not sound it but we're really good friends. We don't have anything in common except friendship, but that's enough. We run together for the Miami Dolphins.

On and off the field. We're always on the run.

That's what disturbs our coach, Don Shula—the running we do off the field.

Shula thinks that me and Zonk are always plotting against him all the time.

We are.

But not always on purpose. Sometimes it just comes out that way. Like the night before our game with the New England Patriots up there last season. We were staying at the Marriott outside Boston, and at nine-thirty we were supposed to be at the team buffet that Shula always has the night before a game. Hamburgers and bottles of beer.

That's his way of getting us back to the motel early for our eleven o'clock room check.

We got to the buffet late. But the hell of it was, we hadn't even left the motel. We stopped to talk to some people in the lobby, then we couldn't find the room where the buffet was. By the time we got there, we had missed Shula's speech. That pissed him off right away.

I'd had a few Jack Daniel's, and when I poured my beer I missed the glass. He really gave me a look.

He just looked, he didn't say anything. The next day, we won. I scored a touchdown and Zonk went over 100 yards. The next weekend, when we were on our charter to New York to play the Giants, he came over to talk to us.

We like to kid around with him, but that wasn't a day to kid around. We could tell just by looking at him, just the way his jaw was jutting, that this was not a day to kid around.

He had an idea that some guys on the team had been fooling around in Boston, so naturally he assumed it was us. Which was true. It was us. But he didn't know for sure.

He told us, "I saw you guys last week at the meeting." But what he didn't know was that Zonk almost ran over one of the assistant coaches driving out of the parking lot. Then he said, "I didn't like the way some guys looked last week. Some had a glint in their eyes."

When he used the word "glint," we knew he knew. We got to the buffet on time that night. Sober, too.

After we beat the Giants, he came around the locker room shaking hands and Zonk told him, "See what staying in the night before the game will do." Shula laughed. That's what I mean about knowing when to kid around with him, and when not to. I respect Shula, even though I'm not on the best of terms with him myself because of the way he played Mercury Morris so much last season instead of me, but I respect him.

You've got a bad attitude, that's all.

Ever since I've been in high school, coaches have been telling me I've got a bad attitude. But even though I dislike the way he handled my situation, I've got to admire him. As far as coaching goes, I've got to respect him.

Maybe you don't have a bad attitude.

Even so, Shula's not the kind of coach you want to win for as much as you want to win for yourself. Because it's easier that way. Winning keeps him off your ass.

That's it exactly. If you win, it makes for an easier life. Because if you lose, Shula goes crazy. Even last season, when we were 17 and 0, he worried about losing.

After we won the Super Bowl, that's the only time he didn't say anything about the next game.

Shula is a helluva coach. His record shows that. Our previous coach, George Wilson, wasn't a coach as much as he was an old player. He was a star end with the Chicago Bears, then he coached the Detroit Lions before becoming the Dolphins' first coach. George was a great guy. You wanted to win for George because he was such a great guy. If he hadn't been fired, if Shula hadn't taken over, it's hard to say if we'd be as good or not. Maybe yes, maybe no.

For actual football knowledge, George wasn't as meticulous as Shula is. And he wasn't as good a sideline coach.

He didn't have the good assistants Shula has, like Bill Arnsparger and Mike Scarry on defense, Monte Clark and Howard Schnellenberger on offense before Howard left to be the Baltimore Colts' head coach.

But the guys really wanted to play and win for George Wilson, because he was such a helluva guy.

George wasn't too concerned with the room check. At one of our first team meetings when me and Jim were rookies, he told everybody, "If you've got something good going somewhere and you're going to miss the curfew, give me a phone call." That's the kind of coach that most football players appreciate, that they want to win for. Just to keep him around.

But his last season, we won three games.

One of those wins was up in Boston after me and Jim

and Jack Daniel's had a big night together. Then on Sunday it rained cats and dogs. The field was a mudhole. On one play, Jim slid through the mud and came up with his face-mask packed with mud. He had mud in his eyes, in his nose, in his mouth. Wet, sloppy mud.

I almost drowned.

"Don't swallow any of that," I told him. "It'll spoil the taste of the bourbon."

The 1969 season was when we began to hang together.

When we were rookies in 1968, we got to know each other at the College All-Star game. When we reported to the Dolphins, we were roommates at training camp and on the road. We got to be pretty good friends, but nothing special.

We had different backgrounds. I grew up near the big city, Zonk was off the farm.

But in our second season, 1969, our personalities started to develop in the environment of pro football. Even though our backgrounds were different, we now had the same griefs and bitches. And we both liked to have a good time. Just go have a few beers, see what was happening.

We never planned anything. We just let it happen.

Those are the best times anyway, when you don't plan anything. Then the Butch Cassidy and the Sundance Kid thing developed, and it stuck.

It gave us identity as a pair. People remembered us together, not separately. I'm Butch.

I'm Sundance. One of the Miami sportswriters, Bill Braucher of the *Herald*, put it on us. I'm always in the locker room early. Bill's usually there too. We talk a lot and I always tell him little things, like the bourbon thing in the mud. I always enjoy a little humor, no matter how tough the situation is. Laughing is important.

When we had a good game against the Denver Broncos a few weeks later, Bill put the nicknames on us. Two guys out to have a good time, no matter what the situation. It was perfect for us. I'd seen the movie four times. I loved it. Me and Zonk always took things as they came, like Butch and Sundance did. It fit perfectly.

Like in Los Angeles, a bunch of Rams jumped on Jim on a sweep. When they finally unpiled, he said to me, "Who are these guys?" Just like they did in the movie.

We put it on a little bit but basically it's the way we are. We didn't have to change our personalities. We could live up to that Butch and Sundance image without trying.

But there's another image that really annoys me. Just because I'm bigger than most running backs, I'm pictured as a brute, a monster. What bothers me is that when little kids come up to me for an autograph, some of them actually look scared, like they think I'm going to grab them and bite their heads off. I hate to see that. Little kids seven or eight who are actually afraid of me. It really appalls me. I like kids. It really bothers me that they're scared to talk to me. And it's only because of a false image created by the image of football. If you're a big running back, you're a brute, a monster.

I've been with Dick Butkus, the Chicago Bears' middle linebacker, and seen people react the same way. Me and Jim were on the *Sports Challenge* TV show and Dick was the mystery guest. After the show, they had a buffet and Dick stopped to talk to somebody in front of a big platter of chicken wings. He didn't realize that he was supposed to keep going along the table; he just kept on talking and chewing on those chicken wings. Nobody had the nerve to tell him to move along, either. They just walked around him without saying a word to him. And those bones from the chicken wings kept piling up.

Another time I was on a plane with Dick and all he wanted to talk about was his little girls and their projects in school and their Easter baskets. At first, I couldn't believe that Dick Butkus would talk about things like that. But when I thought about it, I had to laugh at myself. I had believed his image, too. I think he enjoys it a little though. To tell you the truth, I don't mind grownups acting afraid of me. But with kids it really bothers me, because kids should know that professional sports is something that stems from being a kid. Being a professional athlete is just being a big kid.

But not everybody thinks of me as a brute. Like last season when Dan Dowe, our equipment man, came over to me in the locker room.

"There are some girls outside," Dan said. "About half a dozen of them from a sorority at the University of Miami, and they want a souvenir from you."

"What do they want?"

"One of your jockstraps," he said.

"Give 'em one then."

On a pro football team, no player has his own personal supply of jockstraps. By that I mean the club supplies them. When you take one off, you throw it in a barrel with the rest of the dirty laundry. The next day, there's a clean jockstrap in your locker, but chances are it isn't the one you wore the day before. Actually, there's always two or three jockstraps in your locker. That day I took one of them and handed it to Dan.

"One more thing," he said. "They want it auto-graphed."

I signed it. I'm just sorry I couldn't go out and present it to the girls myself. Dan had to do it because I had to hurry into one of Shula's meetings. But for a bunch of college girls to think of something like that really was cute. They sure as hell didn't consider me to be a brute.

I don't have a "brute" image because I'm not that big. And when I had real long hair, people never thought I was a player.

Jim's really the brute. When he was playing football at Wyoming, he actually bit a guy on the leg. He bit a human being.

We were playing Brigham Young and I had such a bad ankle, I didn't start. But after I got in, I made a long run and this guy tackled me. We went down and in the pileup he started twisting my bad ankle. His legs were near my face and I bit him. On the calf.

How hard did you bite him?

Hard enough that he let go.

That guy probably tells everybody now, "Jim Kiick bit me on the leg." But that's like last season when the Balti-more Colts were losing after all their big years. When we beat them up there, a writer asked me: "Do you have any compassion for Mike Curtis or Ted Hendricks now that they're on a losing team?"

"Compassion, my ass," I said. "How can you have compassion for somebody who's knocking the hell out of you? I have compassion for myself on the football field, and that's it. If you start feeling sorry for another team, that's not part of football. Nobody ever had compassion for the Dolphins in the years when we were getting the shit kicked out of us."

I don't have any compassion for anybody when I'm playing parlor games or cards. I hate to lose at anything. Me and my father and my brother are all the same way. We hate to lose so much that my wife and my mother sometimes won't play with us. I take it very seriously. And if I'm losing, I get sulky. Just like if I'm winning, I get very cocky and smug.

"You wouldn't act like that," my wife always says, "if you were losing."

I just laugh and get cockier and cockier. I'm the same way when I play basketball. I like individual sports more than team sports. Basketball is really my favorite game. Even though it's a team sport, it boils down to each going one-on-one with the guy covering him. I love the challenge of one guy trying to stop me.

I prefer team sports like football, because my teammates are there. I like to hold up my end. Basketball or golf or pool don't interest me as a competitor. If I win, I win. If I lose, I lose. The only exception to that is when I play Monopoly. I go absolutely crazy. My wife, Pam, won't play with me, my parents won't.

I found that out one day at Joe Namath's football camp. Me and Zonk were there as guest instructors.

We had a big Monopoly game going in the house where Joe was living. From the first roll of the dice, I was wheeling and dealing.

One of the guys in the game was Jerry Gialanella, a friend of mine from Lincoln Park who came up to see me. He's a conniver.

He's a cheat.

We had partners—me and Jerry against Zonk and Joe, but Jerry was handling the deeds. Sneaking the deeds really. Zonk finally landed on Park Place but Jerry told him: "Oh, that's Jim's." He'd slipped it to me.

I threw the money in the air. I was really pissed off. Nobody had landed on Park Place and when I finally landed on it, Jerry told me that Jim owned it. Bullshit. I had been watching it for hours. Nobody had landed on it. But even so, we had a great time up there with Joe for a few days. Joe's a helluva guy.

My rookie year, I made the AFL All-Star game but I was in awe of him. He'd just won the Super Bowl with the Jets; he was the biggest thing around. He didn't know me, but he treated me like he'd known me for years. I still look up to him. It's hard for me to realize that I'm playing in the same league that he is.

All the people who knock Joe Namath really piss me off.

Some blonde once told us that he doesn't appeal to her.

She was just getting her rocks off saying that. She would've run through eight lanes of traffic just to hold hands with him. People like that think they're so smart, when they're really so stupid. So many people have the same ego problem, trying to put somebody down when they feel inadequate themselves. That's all she was doing. But she was too stupid to realize that everybody else realized it.

It really pisses me off when people talk about people they don't even know. Especially chicks.

It's too bad some chicks don't have athletics. It really would smarten them up. Some of them try to live the glamour routine all the time instead of just being real. But more and more of them have become real too. If a real chick hears a four-letter word, she doesn't try to pretend she's the Virgin Mary; she understands that some guys talk that way.

People don't realize that athletes are just regular people. They'd rather cut them down, even when they don't know them.

Like with Jim's hair and clothes. I don't wear my hair that way, and I don't wear the mod clothes he does because I don't think I'd look very good with them. I would if I were smaller and a little slimmer, but I'm not. I get a charge out of people who criticize Jim's hair or clothes. What they're really saying is, "You're not like me, so you're an asshole." When you realize that, then you know who the real asshole is.

To me, most of the people who don't say anything about my hair or my clothes, they probably don't like it. But at least they're courteous enough not to say anything. The people who do say something, deep inside, they'd probably love to be wearing wild clothes and long hair, but they're afraid to do it. I have to laugh at that because those people don't have the guts to do what they really, deep inside, would like to do.

We have a lot of fun together. Just doing crazy things, like driving for a couple days.

We just take off. Couple years ago we took off for Cleveland, with a stop in Knoxville.

We stopped there to see Stan Mitchell, who used to

be on the Dolphins with us. He was back in school at the University of Tennessee, but when we got to Knoxville about six in the morning we didn't know exactly where Stan lived. All we knew was that he was in an apartment on the campus somewhere. We drove around the empty campus not even knowing where to go. We finally stopped and walked out into this motel-like court with about a hundred apartments around it. We were hollering "Stan, Stan"—by now it's maybe quarter to seven and people in night clothes are opening their doors and windows.

They were wondering, "Who are these guys?"

The more people we saw looking at us, the quieter our voices got. Finally we stopped yelling. I said, "I don't think he's in any of these apartments," and Jim said, "Yeah, ol' Stan can't be very big around here." Just as Jim said that, a door opened behind him and Stan walked out, not ten feet away.

We had a great day. Stan knew somebody with some white lightning. We mixed it with fruit punch for breakfast, then we went out drinking with him the rest of the day.

And the rest of the night. Then we kept driving to Cleveland to meet Mark McCormack, our business representative. He's the same guy who made Arnold Palmer a millionaire. He doesn't have that good a shot with us but his International Management, Inc., is a good organization. Investment people. Tax people. Accountants. They make life easy for us, but that first day I doubt if Mark McCormack was too impressed.

Ed Keating, the McCormack man in charge of us, showed us around their big office on Erie View Plaza, but we were so tired we were just nodding and trying to keep our eyes open. Then we drove down to see Zonk's family in Stow.

Another time Jim was going to drive from Miami to Lincoln Park and what the hell, it was something to do so I went with him. As soon as he picked me up, he got out and said, "You drive for a while." We stopped a few times for a few beers, but I drove all the way to Washington, straight through.

We always drive straight through.

At any rate, in Washington, he let me sleep while he drove. But when I woke up, we weren't on the New Jersey Turnpike, we were in Gettysburg, Pennsylvania; we were two hundred miles out of our way.

"Why didn't you stop for directions?" I asked him.

And this was exactly what he said to me; he said, "There wasn't a gas station on this side of the road."

Finish the story.

You can finish it.

We were in the middle of Pennsylvania and Zonk said, "How long will it take to get to Lincoln Park from here?"

"About three hours," I said.

"Hell," he said, "when we get to Philadelphia, drop me off at the airport."

"What for?"

"I think I'll fly back to Miami," he said.

He made that whole trip just to fly back.

That's us.

Not us. You.

We really get along good. About the only standing argument we have is when we're on the road—who's going to get out of bed to turn off the TV set, and how much the window is open.

Zonk freezes me out. One morning in Buffalo I woke up with snow on the rug under where the window was open.

Another argument is who's going to answer the phone. We both hate to answer the phone. At home it seems like I can never sit in a chair and just drowse off or never shoot some pool without running to the phone to tell somebody something they should know already.

I seldom answer the phone. When it rings, I tell Alice to say I'm not home. When she finds out who it is, I talk to who I want to talk to.

I really hate talking to people I don't know. Somebody has given them my number and they're calling because the local chapter of something is having a big production. I hate having to turn people down. It seems like a shitty thing to do on the phone.

We appreciate people wanting us but sometimes it's a real pain in the ass.

It puts us in a lot of embarrassing situations. It's really embarrassing to me when people come up and tell me how much they love the Dolphins and how they're such a dedicated fan of mine. I tell them "Thank you," but that doesn't seem very sufficient. At the same time, I don't want to hand them back the same sugar, because then the sugar gets so thick it's like syrup.

That's one reason I always go back to Lincoln Park after the season for a couple weeks. I'm just Jim Kiick there. My friends there like me because I'm just another one of

the guys. Me being a player doesn't mean anything to them.
We just go out and have a good time.

It's nice to be sort of famous, but it's not always easy.
Not that we're complaining. Hell, we're making good money
doing something we enjoy. That's the secret of life. Not
many people are that lucky. We're extra lucky because we're
on a good team, the best, the only one in NFL history ever
to go through the regular season, the playoffs and the Super
Bowl unbeaten and untied. Seventeen and 0.

To me, it's a job with a chance to excel. But the dif-
ference with other jobs is that in pro football people see
you. You might be the president of a company and the
people in that company know you're good, but nobody else
does. In pro football, you're among the best out of every-
body who plays football. And you're on display. People see
you. If you excel, everybody knows about it.

I enjoy the crowd at a game. Our fans especially. Like
when they're yelling "Dee-fense, dee-fense," I'm on the
sideline listening, I'm not even in the game, but I get goose
pimples.

I don't notice the crowd that much except if I've had
a good run and hear everybody cheering. When we played
the Giants in Yankee Stadium last year, I made a couple
good runs and the people were cheering and I knew they
were cheering for me. I heard that. But for all the things
me and Zonk have done in football, a few people will only
remember that we were the guys on the cover of Sports
Illustrated giving the world the finger.

I was the guy, me, Zonk, with the middle finger of my
right hand extended casually across my left leg.

We got a lot of heat on that. The editors at SI claimed

they hadn't noticed it, but I can't believe that.

Their photographer, Walter Iooss, Jr., told us to fool around, that he was going to take a hundred pictures.

We were out there about two hours. Of the hundred pictures he took, in seventy of them we were screwing around. I guess it's possible the editors didn't notice the finger, but we were doing worse than that in some of the other pictures.

We got about a hundred and fifty letters. Most people loved it. They sent us the cover for us to autograph so they could frame it. I got about ten negative letters, all that shit about how I was dragging down the morals of the teenage kids.

One fan sent me a letter, blaming me. He was a high school coach and it was a real snotty letter. He wrote that "I hope your son is proud of you." Alice answered it for me. She wrote him how my son is very proud of me and she's not concerned about little things like that. She reminded him that he was so uptight he didn't even recognize which one was me. It was a good letter.

Most people I talked to didn't even notice the finger until somebody else told them. It was blown out of proportion.

Life's like that when you're known. I really had one happen to me last year. One day at training camp I had a message to call a real estate man on Key Biscayne, the big island in Biscayne Bay where President Nixon has a home. When I got the real-estate man, he said: "Mr. Kiick, your $2,000 check on the house bounced."

"You must be mistaken," I said. "I didn't give you a check for $2,000 on a house or anything else."

"But you rented a $150,000 home here," he told me.

"I'm sorry, but except to go to the beach there, I've never been on Key Biscayne in my life."

"But my secretary recognized you."

"Somebody forged that check," I said.

It turned out that the check wasn't even written on my bank. The guy who was posing as me had rented the house, backed up a truck and stolen the furniture. But that was only the beginning. The next thing I heard was that a guy, apparently the same one, was posing as me and getting paid for making appearances as me. He even was romancing some chick in Georgia as me, but that was his mistake.

I love this one.

He phoned the chick one night and told her he'd be by in half an hour to pick her up, but the girl told him: "How can you pick me up? I'm watching you on TV."

We were playing the Atlanta Falcons in an exhibition game. That really screwed him up and he took off. When he was arrested in Michigan, it developed that he had rented cars out in my name, plus the house. The thing is, he didn't really look that much like me. He had long hair and a mustache but he was short. People will believe what they want to believe. He even had become engaged to the chick as Jim Kiick and when somebody told me that, it really shook me. But then I liked it. Hell, it cleared me of everything I ever did. I could blame everything on him.

When I was in college at Syracuse, a similar thing happened to me. Not quite that serious, but a couple girls were dating different guys who were using my name. It was a bad situation because Pam and I were married then. But these things are good for our marriage because both our wives realize now that these things happen.

Alice went into a health spa once, and when the instructor found out her name she asked if Alice was related to me. Alice told her I was her husband, but the instructor said, "My best friend dated him in Boston at a party." When she got home, Alice asked me about it and I told her, "I don't know anything about it, that must be the same guy who was posing as me." Fortunately, it was the truth. For once I wasn't lying.

Get the hat.

2

Don Discipline

Don Shula is an ass-busting coach. He's like my father. On our farm in Stow, Ohio, if my father told us to build a barn in thirty days, we better have it built in twenty-eight.

But we bust his ass a little bit, too.

That's because of Jim's bad attitude.

Like when we played the Jets in Shea Stadium last year, my friends from Lincoln Park had a big sign they kept waving. "Run Kiick or Trade Shula."

Shula talked about that sign for three days.

He kept telling me, "I saw that sign." Damn right he saw it. In that game I ran the ball a lot and I told him, "You were a little scared of my boys, eh?" I'm not exactly on ideal terms with him, but he's a good coach. The thing I like about him is that he understands you don't have to be a rah-rah player to be a good player. I'm not the rah-rah type. It's just not me. So if I had to put on a rah-rah act, it'd be false. Shula understands that. Like before a game, I'm so relaxed I could fall asleep in the locker room.

I did fall asleep once in the locker room before a game. I was laying on the floor, like a lot of guys do, and I just conked out. The other guys told me later that Shula kept walking back and forth, glaring at me. He didn't know whether to yell at me or not, because he didn't know if I was just relaxed, or if I was tired from staying out. What he didn't know didn't hurt him. Didn't hurt me, either.

Some of our better games have come with a hangover.

I woke up after about a half-hour. I really felt good then. That little nap was just what I needed to be ready for the game.

I don't get involved in the game until I'm out there.

I don't agree with Shula on everything, but I agree with his attitude toward the rah-rah stuff. He's a peptalk guy, but his peptalks are rational, not rah-rah. He's smart enough to know that he can't bullshit bullshitters. We're a happy-go-lucky team. Only a few guys go for that rah-rah stuff. And for them it's good because it's natural. But for me and Jim it would be phony. False rah-rah cracks under pressure because it's something you never believed anyway. Being a football player is like anything else. You've got to be yourself. Some days I don't say much, but most days I clown around because I'm happy. Even though I hate practice, I'm basically happy there. I like what I'm doing. I like being on a winner. I like the guys on the team. I just like being myself. That's what Shula keeps saying. "Be yourself."

Shula is always himself. Always an ass-buster.

When he took over the Dolphins in 1970, the training camps opened a few weeks late because of the labor dispute that year between the NFL Players Association and the club owners. When we finally got to camp, Shula told us:"We've got to make up for lost time. We're going to have four workouts a day."

Four ass-busting workouts. Two in the morning at eight and eleven, another in the afternoon at two, another at night at seven before the sun went down. Sometimes we kept practicing in the dark until he was happy. No other team in pro football ever had four workouts a day before or since. In one of them, I was lined up as a dummy blocker for Bob Griese in a passing drill when Shula shouted at me from about 40 yards away.

"Csonka," he yelled, "what the hell are you doing?"

I figured maybe my shorts had fallen off. Or maybe my two little boys had run onto the field. I didn't know what else he could be shouting about from 40 yards away.

"You lined up a step too wide," he yelled. "If a line-backer had been coming, you'd have been too far out to block him."

Right then I knew I'd better concentrate every second. Because when you least expect it, he'll really bust your ass.

Those four practices a day were brutal. I thought I had reported to camp in pretty good shape. I would've been in good shape if George Wilson still was the coach, but I wasn't ready for Shula's camp. We had an idea he was going to be tough, but he was ridiculous. Back in May, he had a week of workouts. They weren't exactly mandatory.

If you wanted to come, you came.

But you damn well better show up.

Everybody showed up but me. I had the flu. I hadn't been sick for several years but I was then. I hadn't met Shula yet. All the veterans were due one Monday, then the following Monday all the rookies were due along with all the veterans who missed the week before. I was still weak from the flu so I decided to wait a week and go in with the rookies. It was a good decision.

Except that first Monday, when Shula called Zonk's name, one of the guys told him Zonk was sick. When the rest of us chuckled, right away we could see Shula thinking, Oh, oh, this guy's an asshole.

The next Monday, when I did come in, I weighed 248 and Shula really bitched at that. He gave me all kinds of heat, but then I went out and ran a 4.7 for 40 yards. He was all smiles then. He told me, "If you lose fifteen pounds, you'll run a 4.5." I told him, "No way." I lost fifteen pounds and ran a 4.8. He's got a thing about weight.

He's got a thing about hair too, but compared to most coaches he's pretty liberal.

Jim even got away with growing a beard last season. Or what was almost a beard.

I'd cut my hair short because short hair was in again, but I knew that Shula would like my hair short so I had to do something that he wouldn't like. So I grew a beard. He doesn't allow a full beard so I shaved a hole around the bottom of my chin. That way he couldn't claim that I had a full beard.

I wish you'd grown a full beard.

It wasn't worth the hassle. The year Shula took over, he had an orientation meeting. He looked around and saw a couple guys with mustaches and long hair.
  "About hair," he said. "I don't want extremes."
  "What do you mean by extremes, Coach," I said.

Some people thought I had gone to extremes with my hair already, but Shula was pretty calm.

"No beards," he said, "and no hair down to here."

That was reasonable. Right then I liked the guy. I figured he had a good mind if he wasn't letting things like that interfere with his judgment on ballplayers. He's always harassing me about my hair but I think he's just kidding around.

Shula knows that Jim just likes the mod look. He knows that Jim's not trying to defy him with it.

Most coaches would like their players to have crew-cuts. The coach of the New Orleans Saints sure as hell would. J. D. Roberts won't even let players wear sandals to dinner at training camp. Now that's ridiculous. Things like that have nothing to do with how you play football. I can understand a coach not wanting his players to go to extremes, like Shula says. But no sandals at dinner—a coach who demands that is doing it just to do it, not for a reason. Shula's pretty reasonable.

Shula has rules just for discipline.

He thinks it contributes to winning.

It doesn't for me. Football is supposed to be a game of discipline and I'm sure that Shula feels that the more ways he can discipline his players, the more advantageous it is to the team as a whole. On our jet charters, we have to wear a jacket with a shirt and a tie. It's a club rule. Except that I don't see how it helps. It bugs me to wear a tie. I like an open collar. I don't mind wearing a jacket but I don't like to wear a tie. I don't like anything tight around my neck. To say that you have to wear it because we're all going to wear it, that burns me more than anything.

I'm the same way. I don't like to do things I have to

do. That's why I like to do things that are different. Just go a little farther to see how Shula reacts. It's really funny to me to see how he can get upset over little things.

I like to get in arguments with Shula every so often. He knows I like him as a coach and I'm glad we have a winner. But I don't ever want him to think I'm a yes man, that I go along with everything he says just because he's a good coach. There are some guys on the team who pull that shit. They never argue with him. And sometimes they're the guys who bitch the most about him. But when they're face to face with him, they pacify him by agreeing with him. I'm the other way. Alone with him, that's when I really argue the hardest with him. Tooth and claw.

Like in training camp a year ago, I thought he had my weight too low. He had me at 237 but I wanted 240. I couldn't see how three pounds made any difference in camp. It wasn't that I wanted to be 240 during the season. But in training camp, I'm so hot I drink a lot of liquids and I gain weight. As soon as I told him my reason, he jumped up from behind his desk and started talking about how my weight is too high at 240 and to get down to 237. That's when I got mad. I got a few things off my chest. But after killing myself for three weeks, I got down to 237.

That's what I mean. It's easier to do what he says than to have a big hassle with him. But there are times we fool around with him.

I scared the hell out of him one day last season, the Friday before the Giant game. New goal posts had been put up on our practice field. Inside the empty crates were green strips of rubber that looked just like snakeskin. I couldn't resist. I picked up a strip, figuring to have some fun. That's all I think about in practice. Some way to get something happy going, some way to break the monotony because it's so dull. I wandered down near the punting unit with the rubber strip in my hand. I'm not involved in the punting team, so Shula lets me stand around mostly on Fridays because he doesn't want to holler at me every day to make me go over with the rest of the backs.

Shula knew I was there, but he was yelling at the punting team about how not to piss on their shoes or something. Then he walked over to where he saw me holding something in my hand.

"What've you got there?" he asked.

"I found a snake," I said. "Here."

I tossed it at him and he went "Yow." That's just what he yelled. "Yow." I thought he had a heart attack. But it scared him so bad, he didn't get pissed off. He didn't know what to do. He chuckled. Then he walked around looking like he was going to get pissed off. Then he chuckled again. By then he looked lost and everybody was laughing at him. He can't stand that. But he didn't really get mad. I don't know why.

You're his son, that's why. The old Hungarian father-and-son team.

Maybe that does promote a little feeling, the fact that we're both Hungarian and we're both from the Cleveland area. I say shitty things to him all the time and I get away with most of it. Before our game with the Jets in Miami last season, we had a big thing about tickets—a big meeting of the players because all of us needed more tickets. But there was no real solution. Another thing important to this is that Shula thinks everybody on the team is gung-ho about the Dolphins; he thinks that everybody in the NFL would just absolutely want to be on the Dolphins, and that if you're on the Dolphins, there is no way that you'd want to be traded. Anyway, after the meeting about the tickets we were walking toward the practice field, me and Jim and Shula and a few other players.

"Coach," I said. "I've got a solution."

He turned around, really intent to listen, and Jim and all the other players got quiet.

"Trade me and Jim to the Jets," I said. "We'll get you all the goddamn tickets you want."

"You think everything's a joke," he said.

He really was pissed off. Now if I'd said that to him in private, he would've chuckled a little. But with all the other guys around, it really pissed him off because he's always afraid of how he looks in front of the players. It screwed him up a little too because me and Jim talk all the time about being traded. He doesn't know if we're serious or not. He's hoping we're not serious, but anytime he's talking to us I can see him trying to figure out if we're kidding or serious.

Another time we were walking out to practice and he said to me, "You looked faster yesterday than I've ever seen you look."

It had rained the day before, and for Miami it had almost been cold. I guess it was down around sixty, but when you're used to ninety-five it's a big drop to sixty.

"That's what cold weather does for me," I said.

"You like cold weather, eh?" Shula said. "You really like to play football in cold weather?"

"I love cold weather. I really love it."

"I know what you're hinting at," he said. "I know all about you calling Namath and asking him to tell Weeb Ewbank that you wanted to be traded to the Jets when you were holding out. As soon as Joe talked to him, Weeb called me up. I know all about it."

I just grinned at him.

He can't stand that.

Before our Super Bowl game with the Dallas Cowboys, he was surrounded by photographers one day. I told one of them, "I hope you've got a wide-angle lens." We're always busting his balls about him getting fat. He took it good. He laughed and then he went to kick me, playful like. That's just when the photographer took the picture, with him pretending to kick me in the ass.

I love to screw him up. Especially when he thinks I should be concentrating on the game, even an exhibition game.

To be honest, I don't give a damn about exhibition games—the pre-season, the NFL calls it. We were in Washington last year to play the Redskins, and we were walking into RFK Stadium when here came the Redskin cheerleaders. Real fine fillies. One was walking alongside me, with Shula about four feet in front of me. She had trouble with her identification at the gate but I vouched for her. Now we were inside the stadium and I said:

"What's your name?"

I considered that to be a natural, polite, friendly question, but Shula spun around and stared at me. I don't know what he thought I had in mind. In another two minutes I had to be in the locker room.

He doesn't trust Zonk, that's why. He trusts me, but not Zonk.

He doesn't trust either of us. He knows a hell-raiser when he sees one, because he was one himself. When he was a defensive back with the Cleveland Browns, the Baltimore Colts and the Redskins, his teammates used to go get him the night before a game and put him in a car to get back for curfew. Now he's the other side of the coin. He's up every morning for mass and communion. He'd like everybody to believe he's always been this way, but he knows that me and Jim know better. We've heard the stories from guys he played with.

When he gets on me and Jim about slipping out after curfew, he knows we'd like to. With us, the eleven o'clock room check the night before a game isn't if we're going to be checked, it's how many times. Always once. Sometimes twice.

The big thing is not to defy him openly on the curfew. I think he gets a big charge out of guys sneaking around, the cat-and-mouse stuff. Like before the Giant game last year when he reminded us that if anybody missed the curfew, that player was subject to suspension and loss of pay— that was no time to defy him. He had said it, loud and clear. Which meant that he would stick by it. If anybody had been caught that night, Shula is not the kind to say: "Well, now, go back to your room and let's keep it quiet."

No way. After having said it in front of the whole team, he would've stuck by the suspension and the loss of pay. To the letter and to the dollar.

Shula never takes the room check. I don't think any NFL coach does. The assistant coaches always do it.

Tom Keane usually checks us. He's the defensive backfield coach, our only assistant coach who has been with the Dolphins since 1966, the team's first season.

Half the time, when Tom checks, we always have some people in our room.

Tom tells us, "I don't care what you guys do before the room check and I don't care what you do after it, but when I get there I want you guys in the room and I don't want anybody else in there."

We tell him, "The party will be going great, Tom, come in and fix yourself a drink." And he'll shake his head.

But when he does come by and sees some people in there, he won't say, "Everybody out." He'll call one of us outside the door and say, "Look, it's five to eleven, make sure these people are gone." Sometimes he comes back and sometimes he doesn't. But he's got class. He'll tell us, "Now if Shula asks me, I've got to tell him the truth—that you've got some people in your room." We appreciate that.

Monte Clark panics when he sees people in our room.

Monte's our offensive line coach. When he's checking and he sees people in our room, he doesn't know what to do. So he just hides outside in the hall, waiting until the people leave. One time Jim's wife was in the room. We were in New York to play the Jets and Alice had come up for the game. She was sitting in our room when Monte checked, but he stood there, waiting for her to leave. Jim's wife. I mean, no coach should stand there waiting for a guy's wife to leave. But he did.

There were a couple other people there, too, but we weren't having a big party. We were just talking. Monte stood around the corner in the hall, waiting for them to leave.

That's another bitch I have with Shula on discipline. The night Jim's wife was in our room, so were a couple of Jim's pals from Lincoln Park and we were just having a nice conversation. Big deal. Nobody is going to go to sleep at eleven o'clock anyway. You watch TV until you get sleepy, but that might not be for a couple hours. I think being in the room is sufficient, but Shula's order is that

we've not only got to be in our room but that everybody
else has to be out of it.

"It's a ridiculous rule," I told him the next day.

"It's got to be the same for everybody," he said.

"The hell it does," I said. "This was Jim's wife. You've
got to admit, the rule is a little ridiculous in this situation."

"It's got to be the same for everybody," he repeated.

He's got the last word. He's always got the last word.

One time he didn't. One morning last season I was in
the locker room early like I always am. I was getting myself
a cup of coffee when Shula walked in. Just the two of us
were there. None of the other players had arrived yet.

"What's this I read," he said, "about you not liking
practice."

He was half serious and half joking. Which meant that
if I wanted to back off, he'd keep on pursuing it. But if I
gave him some grief, he'd back off. I had talked to some
sportswriters about not liking practice, so I figured that's
what he was talking about. But before he finished telling
me about the article, I told him: "That's the truth. I don't
like practice. You've known me for three years. You know
that I don't like practice."

"It sounded like you were speaking for the whole
team," he said. "You can't do that. You can't speak for
everybody."

"I wasn't speaking for everybody," I said, "but what's
the difference? If you can find two guys on this team who
like practice, it'd be a miracle."

"That's not true," he said. "There are a lot of guys on
this team who like practice."

"Bullshit," I said. "That's just not true. And you know

it's not because you were a player once yourself. You can't tell me that you liked practice."

"I loved practice," he insisted.

"You're full of shit," I said.

Just as I said that, a little too loud too, our assistant trainer, Stan Taylor, walked into the locker room. When he heard it, he looked like he wanted to disappear. I don't think Shula even noticed him because now we were serious.

"I did like practice," he said.

"You weren't practicing for a coach like you," I said. "Who was your coach?"

"Weeb Ewbank," he said, "when Weeb was with the Colts."

"Right there you proved my point," I said. "I've seen TV of the Jets, running around in sweatsuits, no equipment. I wouldn't mind that, either. But there's no way that's going to happen down here with you. There's no comparison. I'd love to run around like the Jets do and have a good time at practice."

"You wouldn't win," he said.

"All right," I said. "You made my point. But that doesn't mean I have to like it."

For once I had the last word.

The reason I don't like practice is that I hate getting yelled at. I feel that I have enough pride in myself to push myself. I'll take instructions or help, fine, but I can't stand somebody yelling at me. I'm not saying it's wrong because I'm sure some guys need to be yelled at, they need to be pushed. That's the main job of a coach, to know the personalities of the players. Which ones to yell at, which ones not to yell at. I think Shula yells at me less than he does at other guys because he knows I don't like to be yelled at.

Like if somebody yells at me, I'll just tell him: "You do it."

Other guys, when they're yelled at, they'll work harder. But that's one reason Shula is a good coach. He knows the personalities of the forty guys on the team.

I agree with the way he pushes some guys, and I agree with some of his discipline, but I don't agree with his out-dated policies like having to stay in training camp.

I'm twenty-six years old and I'm kept in training camp for about six weeks like I was a child or a convict—up at seven for breakfast, practice and meetings until ten o'clock at night, in my room at eleven for the check. I've got a wife and two sons that I'm responsible for, but I'm told that I've got to be in my room at eleven o'clock. That just doesn't set right with me at all.

It's a system designed for children, not adults. If they let me go home at night, I doubt that I'd do anything but go home, have a couple beers and go to sleep.

But the way it is, it makes you want to bust out, to go over the wall, to drink beer and raise hell because you're so fed up with the coach who supervises the system that you want to get back at him. I guarantee you, if at training camp I was told that I could stay at camp or go home, half the time I'd stay in camp without any bitching. Just for the convenience. On the nights I did go home, if the club wanted to phone me there at eleven to make sure I was there, I wouldn't bitch about that at all.

But the way it is, I feel I'm being spoon-fed in training camp. My way, it would be my decision.

The way it is now, the coach and the club are saying, "This is the law, you must obey the law."

Wait and see. In a few years, pro football teams will let guys go home at night during training camp like they do in baseball. And there'll be fewer problems. The way it is now, some guys get a kick out of sneaking out after curfew in training camp. Don't let anybody bullshit you that training camps are like seminaries. They're more like prisons. My all-time favorite pro football story happened at training camp with two guys who were roommates.

Two guys just like me and Zonk.

One of the guys had talked for years about how he always dreamed of what it would be like to have a couple chicks attack him—how instead of trying to romance a chick, a couple chicks would be after him. His buddy decided to set it up for him without the other guy knowing about it. His buddy stashed a couple of chicks in a room so that when the two guys busted out of camp one night, the chicks would be waiting to go through with the gag.

Except that when the big night came, the guy it was set up for didn't go.

He was too tired. Or he had to weigh in the next day. Or something. Whatever it was, his buddy couldn't persuade him to go. But his buddy went over the wall anyway. When he got to where he had the chicks stashed, the champagne was on ice, the whole bit. But he had to tell them that his buddy wasn't coming.

"In that case," one of the chicks said, "let's go down to see him at training camp."

"No way," the guy said. "No waaaay," except that he was beginning to think how brazen it would be. "The hell with it, let's do it. Let's go."

When he drove into the parking lot at training camp, he told the girls:

"That's his room, that one up there. You just go in there and no matter what he does, no matter how he jumps around, you just get him. You just attack him."

He gave them the key and up the stairs they went at

three in the morning, two cute asses in hotpants, giggling and laughing.

The chicks opened the door, sneaked inside and closed it behind them. After about five minutes, the guy got out of the car and went up to the room. When he opened the door, the two chicks were crawling all over his buddy.

"Just like I always dreamed," his buddy said.

It's my all-time favorite pro football story. But something like that could never happen in Don Shula's training camp.

No way.

3

Somebody Who Can't Be Caught

For a fan to really understand what it's like to be a running back, I'd like to have a TV camera in my helmet, and a microphone. It's not just what's there to be seen, but also what's there to be heard.

The noise is great. At the snap, the first noise you hear is the crack of the defensive ends slapping their taped hands against the helmets of our offensive tackles. At the same time, there's the clack of the shoulder pads hitting all along the line and the grunting of the linemen as they collide. It's really neat. I love that noise.

Going through the middle with the ball, you hear all that noise and you see guys being blocked. They're going down with this wild look in their eyes behind their facemasks.

They're clawing and scratching, reaching out at you. But you know they're not going to get you. And you have this tremendous feeling of being protected by your offensive line. You see those guys clawing and scratching but they're walled off and that's a great feeling. If you had time, you'd chuckle, "Ha, ha, you can't catch me." If your blockers have done a good job, you get five or six yards. Maybe eight.

Running a sweep, I'm just trying to get away. But running up the middle, I'm challenging them. I prefer that. Because up the middle, I know they're going to be there waiting.

Watching a sweep, fans can see more of what's happening. But if they could see into the inside, where it's really happening, where the guys are getting the hell knocked out of them, then they'd really appreciate what it's like to be a running back. But they don't see that and they don't hear the noise.

They don't realize how many tackles you're breaking.

Running up the middle is like being a sneak thief. You're stealing yardage. You're defying them. The defense sees you do it but you're still defying them and getting away with it. Eight yards might not seem like much until you put eleven defensive players in the eight yards.

That's my line.

Jim said that originally, but when I said it some writer quoted me. I steal all his best lines.

Eight yards is a long way running up the middle.

Most people don't think of it that way. They just think of it as eight yards. From here to there. Eight yards. Like the length of a room. Shula sometimes thinks of it that way, too. One time at a meeting he bitched at us for not breaking any long runs.

"We can't be content," he said, "with gains of six or eight yards."

All the players just looked at each other and wondered what the hell did he want. But by the time he got it out, he realized what he'd said. He almost cracked up laughing. There are teams in the NFL whose coaches would trade their wives for six or eight yards.

When you're running with the ball, you have eleven guys trying to get you, just you. If you get six or eight yards, you've beaten them.

When you're going through the middle, you don't look at one tackler. You see the whole thing as it's spread out in front of you. And you're looking for open space. Running to daylight, as Vince Lombardi called it. Some of those defensive guys are mountains, 6-6 and 280. You're trying to run between the mountains. But when those mountains fall on you, they knock the hell out of you. When you run against the Kansas City Chiefs, all their players are so big you feel they're all looking down at you. And they really are.

Running is instinct. I don't really watch films of the team we're about to play. To me, a running back can't get that much out of films. Running is something that's natural.

You can get something out of a film for a blocking analysis. Like if I'm leading on a sweep, I want to know if the linebacker will be coming over to force the play. As a blocker, you should have some idea of what to expect.

I just look at films for blocking.

I thought you slept through films.

I do, except for watching the linebackers. Like when I have to block for the passer and the linebacker blitzes, I want to know his style. If he'll try to run over me, or if he'll try to dodge me. Most of them try to run over me but Larry Grantham tries to dodge me. If you know what they're likely to do, then you can cope with it. The rest of the film, I sleep. As a runner, studying films doesn't do me any good. You're not going to run any different against one team than you are against another.

That's right. Situations come up differently every play. You never really know what you're going to have to do.

If a tackler is leaning one way, I'm going to go the other way. The film doesn't show me the situation that I'm going to be in. I have to react to a situation in a split second. Watching films isn't going to help me know when that split second is going to occur.

Coaches look at films and tell you what you should've done. But when you're running, you don't have ten minutes to look at film backwards and forwards and decide. You don't have an aerial view of what's developing here or there. You do what your instinct says.

You don't have time to think, *Well now, I saw this in the film and he did that, so I've got to do this.*

I can't ever remember having anything cross my mind from a film when I'm running. Not even once. When you run the ball, your mind is a blank. You don't think. You react to what you see. There's no time to think. Because if you think, you're caught. That's the nice thing about being a running back. You either have the instinct or you don't.

I think a running back gets more satisfaction out of

doing his thing than a quarterback does. If a quarterback throws a good pass, he still needs somebody to catch it. But when you're a running back, you're more on your own.

Except for your blockers. The day of the big, dumb offensive lineman is all over with. Offensive linemen have to be big, fast, agile, quick. They're no longer just pass-blockers. And they have to be smart. Fans don't realize how intelligent linemen have to be, how they have to work at figuring things out quickly. They've got to work at it so hard that it becomes instinctive.

Like a quarterback, a lineman has to be able to read defenses too.

Linemen don't get the publicity they deserve. I always make it a point to tell the sportswriters something about the offensive line. Not just to pacify them or to be nice to them, but because I believe it. No running back goes anywhere without his linemen.

It was Zonk's idea for us to buy each of the offensive linemen a present after the season.

We got them diamond stickpins after we won the Super Bowl; the year before we gave them huge bottles of champagne. I mean, they were huge.

Those bottles of champagne cost about $100 apiece, but the linemen got that money back for us.

When the Dolphins set the NFL rushing record last season, the linemen were just as excited about it as the running backs were. They knew they were just as important in setting the record. They'd probably like to be running backs but they were blessed with different gifts, like tremendous size and strength. Running backs have to be big and strong, and they have to enjoy the chase, like kids do. If you were a kid who loved to have people chase you, you've got the beginnings of a running back. If you were scared of being chased, there's no way you could become one. It's an inner something that can't be changed. Show me a kid who's ten years old and I'll tell you right away if he can be a running back. That doesn't mean he will be one, but I'll know if he's got the soul of one.

As kids, me and Zonk were like that. We loved to run. But even more, we loved to get chased.

On our farm in Stow, Ohio, somebody was always chasing me. When I'd come in the door, my mom would say, "What's chasing you now?" It was always somebody. Like in the winter we liked to snowball cars, even police cars. They didn't arrest you, but if they caught you, they'd cuff you and send you home. We liked to hide down by this bridge near the road. We'd pepper the cars until somebody called the police. When the police came, we'd snowball their car, too. Then they'd jump out and chase us. Big deal. We wanted them to chase us. That was the fun.

That's the point. Not throwing the snowballs but knowing that you're going to get chased, knowing that you possibly could get caught. But deep inside, you know that you can't get caught, that you'll get away. When we played tag as kids, some kids hid. Not me. I wanted to be chased.

It wasn't just the policemen chasing me. Even when I was alone, I always imagined there was a gang of guys chasing me, to do me in. You can always run faster when somebody is chasing you. With the police, you always knew which one of the cops was after you, and you knew that if he caught you, he really would cuff you around. Then you could run like the wind. I remember running on snow in sneakers and being amazed how fast I was going. When you're a kid, you can run forever.

One time in Lincoln Park, me and another kid, Sheldon Sewell, were goofing around on a little bridge over the Passaic River when an older kid came paddling down in a kayak. He was bigger than us but we knew he wasn't fast, so we started throwing dirt bombs at him. He got out of the kayak and started chasing us ... and he chased us ... and he chased us. We found out later that he was on the cross-country team. He finally caught us and beat the hell out of us.

When we played hide-and-seek on the farm, I always was the last one caught. Nobody liked to chase me because they knew I'd run right through anything. If there was a big brier patch, that's exactly where I'd head. I didn't mind running through a brier patch. I'd gone after cows into them. To run through a brier patch full blast was nothing. It didn't hurt. But other kids wouldn't do it because they'd get scratched up.

Out where I lived, we ran mostly in the town. That's different. You've got to know the backyards and the back alleys.

Damn right it is. One time I was about thirteen, old enough to ride my bike into town. All my life I'd run in the woods and the fields. But now I was in town with my buddies from school, running down alleys and around houses. Some cop chased us down an alley into a backyard and I took what I thought was a shortcut across the yard. I was going full tilt when a clothesline snagged me across the neck and flipped me on the ground. I didn't know what hit me. That cop caught me and cuffed me. He had me by the shirt but I took off anyway.

My shirt ripped right down my back. He started to run after me but I put a helluva move on a rose arbor, one of those big fan deals with the thorns on it. I just brushed it and cut my arm, but that cop hit that thing full blast. Whack, crash, he went down with it. I thought I was away clean. But when I went to run through the garden there, the lady had quart milk bottles over her flowers. I barrel-assed into about three of them. I got all cut up. I got away, but I'd learned that running in town was different than on the farm.

The more you got caught, the more you wanted to do it again. Just to see if you could get away the next time.

On the farm, we used to sleep out sometimes, me and a few other kids. But sleeping out wasn't enough. We had to do something, too. We took tomatoes and eggs with us, as many as we could carry. Two or three kids were behind one haystack, and two or three behind another, and you had to run between them to see if you could dodge the tomatoes and the eggs. Many times I got hit splat in the face. But it was always a dare to see who could run across there.

It's still a dare. Me and Zonk are still really kids, doing the same thing we did as kids. It's still the same feeling.

It's a dare that you can't get three or four yards, or the first down when you need it, or the touchdown when you're close.

If you get as many as five or six yards, or eight or ten, or really break a long run, then it's really great because the defensive players are so frustrated. I love to get up after a good run and see the defensive players with that disgusted look and hear them saying, "What happened? . . . How the hell did that happen? . . . Whose man was that?" You chuckle to yourself because they're trying to stop you and they can't.

Inside, a running back feels like he's somebody who can't be caught, who's always got the edge. He's the gambler who's always got the odds going for him. He's got tremendous confidence. One way or another, he knows he's going to get the touchdown or the first down. You've got to feel that you can do it. If you have the feeling that you're going to be stopped, you will be.

It's knowing you can do it. Like when we're near the goal line and the play calls for me to carry the ball, the whole team feels that this play will score a touchdown. So if I don't score, I've let all these people down. I don't want to do that, so I know that I just have to score. Anytime we're inside the 10-yard line, I always feel that I should score on the play. I don't always do it, but I always feel that way.

The guy trying to tackle you feels he's going to stop you, so it's really the guy with the most will power.

Like when I was a kid playing sandlot football, I just thought I was so good I didn't try to avoid people. I wanted people to try to tackle me because I knew deep inside that I could get away. In sandlot football, there was hardly any passing. As a runner, you were the center of attraction.

You've got to be a little bit of a show-off. I enjoy it when I hear the fans yelling when I'm running. It's a great feeling.

When we used to go swimming, we'd play touch football too. That's almost all passing. But I caught passes just to run the ball.

We had a swimming place in Stow, a gravel pit they

had fixed up with sand and a little concession stand. I used to love to go there to play touch football. But talking about being a little bit of a show-off, I was about fourteen and I was just itching to impress the girls. My future wife, Pam Conley, was one of them. All the girls were sitting around on the sand, putting on their suntan oil, and I loved to play touch football in front of them. They were watching and they knew we were performing for them. Nobody said anything but everybody knew.

I think a good running back always knows where he's going without thinking about it.

It's a gift. Like when I was at Syracuse, a guy I knew who was studying to be a psychiatrist, he told me, "You're in a certain group of people who are always banging their hands on things as they walk through rooms. You wouldn't be able to describe a room to me as well as you could tell me how many steps it is from here to there." He's right. Like when I get up in the middle of the night, I'll walk through the house without turning a light on.

I can do that, too. But one time Alice fooled me. I got up one night really hungry. Between the living room and the kitchen in our house, we have sliding doors. They're usually open. But that night they weren't. I walked right into those doors.

Or when the kids leave those little toy cars around the house. I've stepped on one, jumped up in the air and come down on another one, jumped up and come down on a third one. And they're not nice little soft convertibles, they're little trucks with sharp points sticking out. One of those points stuck right in my heel once. I was hopping around the house in the dark, trying to pull it out, when I hopped on another one.

I don't step on things like that. As soon as I touch it, I'll jump away. As soon as I touch it, I'm off.

That's a good point. You watch a good running back, or a running back who's been around awhile, like Bill Brown of the Minnesota Vikings, very seldom do you ever see him get hit with both feet on the ground, or even with one foot planted. As soon as he sees the impact coming, he jumps, he breaks contact with the ground. He wants to be in the air, because then he's less likely to get hurt. Like when I go to hit a defensive back who's coming at me, I'll take a long stride. I want to hit him in between strides.

Zonk just wants to hit him. Zonk is the only running back ever to get a 15-yard penalty for a personal foul. On himself.

We were playing in Buffalo a few years ago and I got through the line. I figured I was finally going to get a long run but one of their safetymen, John Pitts, came running up to stop me. He was straight up, coming in at about a forty-five-degree angle from the right side. I always carry the ball in my left hand. So my right arm was free.

Zonk leveled him with a forearm shot.

Forearm, my ass. It was a right cross.

But nobody ever taught me to take that long stride when I saw a defensive back coming at me. Even in high school, I never hit a guy with my head down, driving. I was always gliding. It's something you either do naturally or you don't.

It's another instinct. Half the time you don't know who's there, but you feel the guy coming at you.

As great as he was, Gale Sayers didn't glide much. I don't know if that was because he had so many moves, or if it was because his legs were always spread out. But he got hit a lot when he was pushing off into his stride. That's the worst possible time. His first knee injury, he was running a sweep and he had one leg planted when Kermit Alexander tackled him across the knee on the leg that was planted. Maybe he just had weak knees. But it seemed like he was always getting caved in when he had one of his legs planted, trying to push one way or another.

If I could go into a store and buy something to make me a better runner, besides speed, it would be longer strides. I've never been able to run with long strides. And if I could be like any runner, it would be like Gale Sayers. He cut at full speed. Not short choppy steps, he cut without shortening his stride. It looked so beautiful. But the most amazing thing to me about Sayers is that he always ran great in the mud. Because of his long strides, you wouldn't think he could. The game when he scored six touchdowns as a rookie, that was in the mud.

But when Gale took his long strides and cut, he'd cut flatfooted. He didn't cut on his toes. He'd put one foot down, his ankle would bend real hard and his foot would be almost at a right angle to his body, and he'd cut with a long stride to that side. Most guys push off their toes but that shortens your stride. Anytime I saw Gale on TV or in films, he always had that foot planted. I really believe that's what finished him. When he got hit with that foot planted, his knee took the force of the tackle. With his foot planted, his knee had no give to it. The force of the tackle tore his knee apart. That's how most serious knee injuries occur.

O.J. Simpson is the closest thing now to what Gale Sayers was. O.J. has the same long strides and he cuts the same way.

When he first gets the ball, O.J. is a lot more faky than Sayers was. Sayers would fake a tackler once, maybe twice, then go. O.J. will play a cat-and-mouse deal with you, trying to triple-odd fake you back and forth.

O.J. comes off the ball almost at half-speed, waiting to see what's developing. Sayers just took off. If there was a hole, he'd go. Otherwise, he'd make one move and go.

Larry Brown is definitely a great back, but I think the Redskins use him too much. He's playing a rougher game than he's capable of. From what I've seen, he's really tearing himself down with all those carries. He doesn't have the weight and the size to handle the number of carries he had last year—285 in the first twelve games. They had to rest him for the playoffs. He gets hit awfully hard on his second effort. He's not that big a guy to hold up under that pounding.

As much as I'd like to copy Sayers or O.J. or Larry Brown, there's no way. You run like you run.

I'm described as a bulldozer, a battering ram, but I resent that. You can't just be big and do it. I don't make what you'd call a cut, but I do make a move. Not a move on somebody, but an adjustment to the hole, to that open space. Just a juke to hit the hole, then I go straight for the hole. As for putting a move on somebody downfield, I don't, but that's not because I don't know he's there. For me, there's just no place else to go but at him.

I slide. I don't make any sharp cuts. I come up to the line and slide along. I take whatever hole is there. When I get hit, my knees churn, but before that, they're just low and sliding. Like when you see John Brockington, his knees are going all the time. He gets a lot of power that way. But that's not my style.

I look for Brockington to get a bad neck injury or a bad head injury. He puts his head down too much. I think Brockington is more of a battering ram than I am. When you drop your head, not only can't you see, but your neck can't absorb much of a shock. You've got to keep your head up. I'll drop my head maybe two or three times a game. Brockington drops his head every time he's slowed down. When he knows he's going to be tackled, he ducks his head. Someone's going to hit him head-on and he's going to lose the collision. Just like that defensive back with the Cincinnati Bengals that he hit, Ken Dyer, lost the collision, paralyzed with a neck injury. They both ducked their heads and Dyer lost because Dyer was a lot lighter. Brockington is going to hit somebody who's bigger than he is, and it's going to work the other way. He also runs with his knees high. He's always got one foot planted.

Jimmy Brown was the exact opposite of Brockington in style. People couldn't understand why Jimmy Brown was so good because he never lifted his knees. But he was a slider. His legs were so powerful, when he'd get hit the tacklers would bounce off.

Jimmy Brown was the perfect combination of power, brute force, a little bit of speed and a little bit of finesse. He ran with his feet low. He almost dragged his feet. Every time he ran he'd hit somebody, but he never hit anybody head-on, always at an angle. At the last second, he'd hit a tackler at an angle and slide past him. He had the weight and the speed to do it. And he had tremendous balance.

His mental drive was fantastic. It seemed like he simply would not allow himself to be denied.

Mental drive is the biggest asset a running back can have. It's more than getting the first down or the touchdown. It's saying to himself at the beginning of the season, I'm going to play the whole season, no matter what. It's being relentless, just being more shitty than anybody else on the field. It's knowing that you're going to be the winner at the end of the season. It's not dedication. That's a coach's word. It's more than that. It's being able to look good personally. Screw everything else.

Jimmy Brown had it.

That's what made Jimmy Brown super. People talk about this back or that back being a real professional back because of his skills and his determination. But when I think of a real professional back, I think of a back who's real durable, a back who's always there. Franco Harris looks to be that type.

Emerson Boozer is a great back. He's been hurt a lot but he sticks his nose in there, he's powerful when he gets hit, he's got great moves, he's a good blocker and he can catch the ball. Another great back is Carl Garrett. He's a completely different type of runner than anybody else. He's really a unique runner.

Garrett never runs the same way twice.

He's powerful for a small guy but he doesn't run with short, choppy steps. Lots of times he reverses his field. Looking at him, he doesn't look that good, but he breaks a lot of tackles. He's got a lot of speed but he doesn't look like a speed back. His legs are moving all over. He's a strange back to watch. He's not a fluid runner. He looks like he's not going to get anywhere. But he's powerful and quick. He always manages to get away.

Leroy Kelly is a dancer. But he's one of the few durable dancers. He's hardly ever missed a game.

Kelly is something like Sayers was. Kelly has long strides too, but not until he breaks loose. Sayers ran with long strides even before he broke loose. When he gets the ball, Kelly likes to juke a lot, then take off.

One of the most intelligent runners I've ever watched is Ed Podolak. Just the way he moves, he knows the situations.

Podolak probably isn't as good a natural runner as O.J., but he's got that instinct. He knows where to go, when to go.

If he runs a certain play, he knows two or three alternatives will develop. When he starts into the play, he's gliding and looking, waiting for one of the alternatives to develop. As soon as he spots it, he makes a very definite directional change. It's not really a cut. He just knows which way to turn his momentum. And he's got tremendous heart. He's really into football. He knows he's the type of runner who's not going to burn 80 yards, but every time he gets his hands on the ball, he's really determined to rip something off.

Podolak looks sometimes like's he's not getting anything done. He's not real fast. He's not that big. But he gets it done.

Floyd Little gets it done too. He's a choppy runner. When you think he's right there to be hit, he's not. He runs in choppy steps in tight. But when he gets into the open, he'll lengthen his stride. He runs on his toes, he doesn't run flatfooted. He's got quickness more than speed. He uses his quickness inside. He'll give a tackler a jab with a shoulder to make it look like he's going one way. But as soon as the tackler goes that way, he slides off and misses him.

Mike Garrett is quick. He's a darter. He never gives a

tackler a good shot at him. His feet are always moving so quick. And he's really strong too. He's a muscular little guy. Heavy legs.

John Riggins's legs are really heavy up in the thighs but he's got spindly bones in his knees and ankles. I can tell by the way he looks in his gear that he's just not heavy-boned. He's probably the fastest of the big backs. Marv Hubbard is a heavy-legged runner like me. I like to watch Hubbard because he makes the same quick adjustment to the hole that I do. Riggins does that too. I really appreciate that in a big back.

Another good back is Ron Johnson, strong and fast. Duane Thomas was a good back when he was playing, but I don't think he played that many years to be a great back. He was good, but nothing tremendous. Not to me. I think all the publicity he got for not talking made people think he was a better back than he really was. Calvin Hill is a good back, but of the backs that were on the Dallas Cowboys when they beat us in the Super Bowl game, I loved to watch Walt Garrison. He's clawing and scratching all the time for extra yards.

Garrison is a tough runner. If you're willing to come in and hit him, he's willing to hit you.

But when Garrison is battling for extra yards, it seems like he's giving out the punishment. When some backs do that, they're vulnerable to get hit. But when he's doing it, he's still giving out punishment.

Duane Thomas struck me as not having any heart for football. He had so many bad personal experiences that he didn't care about being a great football player.

Like the Super Bowl game against us, he had 94 yards.

Some people were saying he should've gotten the Sport Magazine car as the most valuable player. But to me, if it wasn't Roger Staubach, it was Garrison who deserved the car. Half the time when Duane Thomas was running, he had a hole that was unbelievable. Most of the time Garrison didn't have a hole and he still made yardage.

Garrison isn't going to make the fancy-Dan run. But he's going to hurt you more during the game than the back who makes one long run.

The fancy-Dan run doesn't interest me. I believe that the shortest distance between two points is a straight line. Running a sweep, once you get around the corner, fine, but until you do, you've run 10 or 15 yards without gaining a yard. Going up the middle, you're gaining yards and you're going straight toward the goal line.

But every running back is aware that he's running on ice. He never knows where the thin ice is, where the big injury is waiting for him. But inside him, a running back really believes that he can't be injured. He knows that he's going to have injuries, but never one that'll cripple him, never one that'll finish him.

If you believe you can be injured, that's when you're through as a running back.

When you start to think about being hurt, when you start worrying about it, that's when the guy with the sickle will be running behind you and you'll see him every turn.

You have to run like you did as a kid. Just run. Not think about getting hurt.

As a kid, I ran through herds of cows, I ran through

creeks. And if I fell down, I came up running. I never laid there moaning that I was hurt. I came up running. Like when the other kids wouldn't run into the brier patch because they didn't want to get all scratched up, I never thought of being scratched up as being hurt. Being hurt was a broken leg.

4

Nobody Ever Says He's Sorry

Injuries happen. They have to. We're not playing chess. But in virtually every case an injury is an occupational hazard, not a deliberate thing. People are always asking me if pro football is dirty. I tell them, "No, it's not." In the NFL, it's I'm out to do a job, the other team is out to do a job. I try hard, they try hard. It's not, I'm going to kill you because I hate you. There are a few exceptions. Mike Curtis is supposed to be a nice guy off the field but I don't like the way he plays. He mouths off and goes wild. Ben Davidson is like that, too. He nailed Bob Griese once. He nailed Joe Namath another time. To me, there's no need for it. If a man plays good tough football, I'll be the first one to congratulate him, but I don't think a dirty player has the respect of any other player.

You'd think a player would have the intelligence to rise above being dirty.

I never remember me or Zonk losing our temper. I know that I never did.

I did once. Against the Oakland Raiders one time, the whistle had blown but one of their players hit me late. I don't even remember who it was. But he hit me so late, it really pissed me off. I just threw him down. It happened near our bench and Shula hollered at me. But when we saw it in the films, he laughed about it.

If you get pissed off all the time about things like that, you're going to forget what you should be doing in the game.

One guy who's a good guy off the field but a nasty guy in a game is Bubba Smith. He really plays football with temper.

But there are only a few guys like that. Against most teams, it's an enjoyable game. Like the Jets—after a game they're the first ones to come up and congratulate you. After our game with the Jets in Miami last season, Gerry Philbin told me: "If anybody goes all the way besides us, I'd like to see you guys do it."
Little things like that make you feel good, knowing that he respects you.

I enjoy playing against the Chiefs because I know a few of their defensive players from the Pro Bowl game—Willie Lanier, Bobby Bell, Buck Buchanan, Curley Culp. In a game, Curley Culp will knock the hell out of me but then he'll help me up. It means something without really meaning anything. One of my really favorite guys is Willie Lanier, their middle linebacker. When we line up for a play, we're looking right at each other, only a few yards apart. Early in the game I like to give him a big grin. He'll grin back. I respect defensive players. I don't get up slowly every time, like Larry Brown does or like Jimmy Brown used to do, so that the defensive players wouldn't know if I was hurt or not. I'm not worried that if I get up slow, the defensive guys will know they slowed me down. If a defensive guy knocks the hell out of me, I tell him. Like against the Giants last season, I was laying under a pileup.

"If you had let go of my foot," I told Jack Gregory, "I wouldn't have a dozen broken ribs now."

He had been hanging onto my foot, slowing me down, and John Mendenhall had come across and buried himself in my ribs. Gregory knew what I meant, and he slapped me on the helmet, laughing. Mendenhall laughed, too.

When we play the Jets, and John Elliott tackles me, I always tell him, "Way to go, John." Or when Larry Grantham says to me, "You'll never beat me on that pattern," I tell him, "Don't bet on it." I don't hate them.

Just the same, when my career as a running back is over, I'd like to try to be a defensive end for a couple of years. Just to get even.

The only reason I'd like to play defense is that you can walk from the huddle to where you line up. On offense, the coaches always tell you to run to where you line up, to look like you're hustling. But you can't get nowhere then. You ain't got the ball. But running with the ball, that's what I enjoy.

I even enjoy the bumps and bruises the day after a game. It makes me feel like I've been involved.

Definitely. If you're not sore the next day, you haven't contributed what you should've. If you're feeling good, you haven't done much.

I enjoy being tackled hard and clean. I really do. But sometimes it's ridiculous.

Like the time in Minnesota last season when Zonk got leveled. I mean, really leveled.

I had circled out for a third-down pass from Bob Griese and I was looking back for the ball. Out of the corner of my eye, I saw Roy Winston, one of the Viking linebackers, coming at me as I turned for the ball. I knew I had to go for the ball, because if I didn't go for it and he did, he'd intercept and probably go all the way. But what I didn't know was that he was going for me, not the ball. Just as I got my hands on it, his helmet went through the base of my spine.

As big as Zonk is, Winston had so much momentum he ran right through him. Zonk went down but Winston kept running, still on his feet. I couldn't believe he was still on his feet.

I couldn't believe the pain. I'd dropped the ball, so when we came off, I just lay down in front of the bench, face down. My back hurt so much it was numb. I really thought I'd cracked a vertebra. All of a sudden, I heard this voice above me.
"You can't get hurt. You've got to go."
Don Shula. The coach had diagnosed it.
"I don't want to hear your shit," I told him. "I think my goddamn back is broken. Screw the game."
"Take it easy," he said. "Take it easy."
But about thirty seconds later, it stopped hurting. I got up and started moving around. The next series, I felt good enough to go back in. It didn't even ache or throb. As it turned out, it was only a bad bruise. My back was stiff the next day, but no more than usual. I'd never used a pad where Winston hit me, but I've used one there ever since. I've been hit a lot of times in the back and in the ribs,

usually after I've been stopped, but I'm still standing up, hanging there, and the second or third tackler nails me.

It's usually the second or third guy who hurts you. You're ready for the first guy, but not for the others.

So many times when I'm hit like that, I know they've knocked the wind out of me. I can't breathe. But I know the feeling so well, I know exactly how long it'll be before it goes away. I just hold my breath. I'm sure Jim knows exactly what I'm talking about.

On those plays, I wish I was a quarterback. When a quarterback is held by one leg, he just drops. He just looks for a place to fall.

One guy's got you by the head and shoulders, another guy's got your feet, and you're hanging there at a forty-five-degree angle. Your whole back is exposed and there's a 265-pound defensive lineman who's been dreaming about it, and here he comes. One time at Syracuse, when we were playing West Virginia, one linebacker had me by the shoulder, another linebacker had me by the other shoulder, and a lineman had me by the feet. I was just hanging there when I saw a defensive back coming at me as hard as he could, aiming his helmet at my sternum. When he was a couple yards away, I jerked my weight for all it was worth. I moved just enough. He hit his own linebacker in the back. That linebacker went down screaming. I loved it. Just a few inches, and that linebacker was screaming instead of me.

"I'm sorry," the defensive back said. "I'm really sorry."

I thought, You son of a bitch, you wouldn't say you were sorry if you'd hit me.

Nobody ever says he's sorry.

Those helmets are weapons.

One time at Wyoming, we were playing New Mexico and a guy hit me in the stomach with his helmet just before I fell over him for a touchdown. All of a sudden, I felt sick and I just lay there in the end zone. The trainer, Jack Aggers, came running out.

"Are you all right?" he asked me.

"I don't think so," I said. "I think I'm going to get sick."

"No you're not," he said.

"I think I am. I really think I am."

"No you're not," he said.

I'd had onion soup the night before at dinner. I hate onions but I like onion soup. The trainer had me up on one knee by now.

"C'mon, get up," he said.

"I think I'm going to get sick."

"No you're not," he said.

All of a sudden, I threw up. All those onions came up that had been in the onion soup.

I bet he didn't say "No you're not" anymore.

I told him, "I warned you." But getting hit in the stomach by a helmet is like getting hit there by a bowling ball. It's about the same size. And it's got even more weight behind it.

But helmets aren't the big problem with injuries. Artificial turf is.

The bruises you get on artificial turf, you'd never get on a grass field.

The bruises go to the bone more. I've needed an operation after each of the last two seasons—for bone chips in an elbow and for calcium deposits in a big toe. Each one was caused by banging my elbows and toes on the Poly-Turf field in the Orange Bowl where we play our home games or in other stadiums with artificial turf. Of our twenty-three games last year, including exhibitions, we played fifteen on artificial turf.

To me, playing on artificial turf is like playing on a throw rug over asphalt. It's that hard.

I'll take grass any time. Even muddy, it's better than Poly-Turf or AstroTurf or Tartan Turf.

After a game, I like my uniform to be dirty. On artificial turf, your uniform's so clean it looks like you've been playing in your living room. Our first two years in the Orange Bowl, there was grass in there. But it's a city stadium. With the Dolphins, the college teams and the high school teams, it has about forty football games a year. So the city decided it would be less wear and tear on the field if Poly-Turf was installed.

But it turned out to be more wear and tear on the players.

Like last season when Bob Griese dislocated his ankle. If it had happened on grass, there would've been more give. He probably would've had a bad sprain, but not a dislocation.

Nobody really tested artificial turf. They just put it in.

They're testing it on the players. We're the guinea pigs.

It wasn't bad the first year in 1970, but the next year it was so worn it was slippery. Watching films of a game against the Jets, our coaches counted fifty-nine slips and falls. Last year they put in a new rug, but this one was slippery when it was wet. They're still experimenting with it.

The thing that typifies the whole situation is what happened when the Rams played the Cardinals in St. Louis on a cold day late last season. To make sure the AstroTurf didn't get icy, they put a chemical on it to keep it from freezing. Great, except that the chemical was so strong it burned some players right through their jerseys. Nobody thought about how strong the chemical was; they just used it. Almost everything in our society is tested before it's used. But nobody ever tested artificial turf over a period of time to see if it was hazardous to football players. In the meantime, the players are getting busted up, burned, bruised. What the people responsible for installing artificial turf in each stadium really have been saying is, "Let's test it on the players." If it happens to end your career, tough shit. But the most expendable part of the NFL is the players. The owners always can get new players. Every year the owners draft 442 players, like they were harvesting a crop of wheat or corn.

Not that we're really complaining. There are people in this world with really serious injuries. People in hospitals who'll never get out.

I got a perspective on injuries when I went to Vietnam after the 1971 season with a group of NFL players. In the hospitals there, I saw guys with more than injuries. Maimed guys with their legs blown off, their arms blown off. Some were in tremendous pain that had them almost out of their heads. I started thinking about my Poly-Turf toe and about how sportswriters were doing stories about it, and here was a kid in a bed with his face shot off. They were building him a new face from cartilage. Another kid had a drawerful of shrapnel that had been removed from all over his body.

"I'll be out of here in six weeks," he told me. "I'll be back in the field two weeks after that."

Talk about dedication to football, this guy was dedicated to getting back in the field to get even with whoever shot him. As he talked to me, he was holding some of the shrapnel in each hand. Then he said: "You guys did pretty good until you played the Cowboys in the Super Bowl."

I didn't know what to say to him about that. I mean, hell, he was feeling sorry for *me*. Then he said: "I don't think I could play football. I couldn't take all the pounding."

"Are you bullshitting me," I said. "In the NFL, nobody shoots bullets."

That's what I mean about perspective. I've had my nose broken ten times. People think I'm tough because I keep playing with it when it gets broken again. It's not that big a deal, especially when it's been broken ten times. The first time, I was a kid on the farm, I was putting a bucket of water into a manger and when I set it down, it startled a steer who was grazing. The top of his head came up and caught me across the nose. It wasn't that bad. It was flattened a little and it bled a little. Made my eyes water. But it didn't hurt that much. I had a shiner but I didn't go to a doctor. I just pinched it back up. It wasn't any big thing. I broke it again wrestling in high school. The other times, I broke it playing football—four in high school and college, four with the Dolphins, but that's mostly because I like a big helmet. I like my helmet to come down over my eyes to shade them. But sometimes it gets jammed across the beak of my nose and breaks it. One time it was even funny. It was really bleeding bad, making bubbly noises, pouring out in a steady stream. We were in the huddle, and when I leaned over to hear the call I bled all over Marv Fleming's pants and shoes. I noticed Marv's eyes getting bigger and bigger, like he was going to upchuck. I turned the other way and bled on Jim's shoes. Jim enjoyed it. It made him think he was in the game.

I've really been fortunate. I've never had any serious injuries to speak of.

Don't believe it. Jim's had a broken ankle, a broken finger, a bad back, a bad knee. He's had more injuries than most of the guys on the Dolphins. But he's hardly missed a game. Once a writer described him as injury-prone and he really got pissed off, because even when he's been hurt he's almost always played.

Two broken ankles, but one I didn't know I had. It couldn't have been bad.

That's right. The broken ankle he knew about, he got playing basketball.

On the Dolphins we have a basketball team in the off-season. One night we were playing a high school faculty team. When those teachers hear the people cheering, they think it's their old high school days. They get a little excited. On a loose ball, I jogged over to get it but a faculty guy dove for it and landed on my ankle. I heard a crack, but I finished the game. The next day, I couldn't walk. X-rays showed it was broken. They also showed the ankle had been broken once before but I couldn't figure out when. Dr. Herbert Virgin, our team doctor, put a big walking cast on my leg.

"Now stay off it," he said.

I tried to play tennis but I got chased off the court. The next week I went up to Lincoln Park and played basketball on the asphalt courts. With the cast on. Tore the hell out of it. The metal walking part got so jammed into the cast, it was hurting my arch. My toes were all scratched. The cast was really a mess. The day I went back to Dr. Virgin to have it removed, he said: "What is this? Whatever happened to the cast?"

"I guess they don't make 'em like they used to."

The ankle healed all right. But sometimes an injury can make you change your style. Like ever since I broke my right index finger a couple years ago, I haven't been able to carry the ball in my right hand. I prefer to carry it in my left hand but until I broke the finger, if I was running around the right side, I switched the ball to my right hand so I could use my left hand to stiff-arm a tackler. When my finger was broken, I kept playing but I had to carry the ball in my left hand all the time. I got so used to it, I don't switch the ball to my right hand anymore. I don't know if it's psychological or what, but I just can't do it.

Jim doesn't stiff-arm much anymore.

The defensive players keep getting bigger and stronger. It's harder to stiff-arm now.

Stiff-arming is how Jim broke his finger.

I don't know how I broke it, I really don't. In college and high school, I used to stiff-arm tacklers and get away with it. But in the pros, they just grab you. I don't even stiff-arm with my right arm going around the left side anymore. I don't want to take a chance on fumbling.

For a running back, there's no greater feeling than gaining yards. But there's no worse feeling than realizing that the ball got away.

Fumbling is the most embarrassing thing that can happen to a running back. The other guys on offense are pissed off at you because you've lost the ball. The defensive guys are pissed off at you because they've got to go back in. Me and Zonk have been lucky. We haven't fumbled much. But the way me and Zonk run, we try to protect the ball so a tackler doesn't have a good shot at it.

We don't fumble much because we don't want to see ourselves fumble on Tuesday when we see the films of the game.

It's luck, too. If a guy hits you the wrong way, you're going to fumble no matter how you protect the ball.

I always carry the ball in my left hand. I have a mark on my arm, on the bicep right above the elbow where I jam the back nose of the ball into the skin. That's why I don't wear elbow pads. I want to feel the back nose of the ball in my arm. And when I'm running, I lean over the ball, to protect it. My fingers are around the front nose of the ball, the back nose is dug into my arm, and the backside of the ball is jammed against my ribs. I like to feel the ball against my ribs.

I usually hold it in my left foream. I used to carry it with two hands, almost like a basketball, but not anymore.

I'm right-handed but I don't feel I can grip the ball with as much strength in my right hand as I do in my left hand. As a kid, I swung a baseball bat left-handed, too. My dad couldn't get over it. My two boys are the same way.

I used to hit and throw with either hand because my mother told me it increased your brainpower to be ambidextrous.

Get the hat.

Tell my mother to get the hat.

My dog ate tomatoes and you're saying that it increased your brainpower to be ambidextrous. Get the hat.

Tell my mother to get the hat

I know this, that carrying a football with two hands on it can be dangerous. With two hands on the ball, you don't have a hand free to break your fall. The worst injury I've ever had was a concussion I got that way in my rookie year. I was carrying the ball with both hands against the Bills in Miami, and I got hit high and low. With both hands on the ball, the way I fell, I landed on the side of my helmet. I'm lucky there wasn't Poly-Turf there yet. The impact, I learned later, broke a blood vessel inside my head. Our trainer, Bob Lundy, helped me off the field, then I collapsed in his arms. He stretched me out near the bench. I remember seeing Dr. Virgin's face above me. He had his hands in my mouth to make sure I didn't swallow my tongue. Lundy had an oxygen cone over my nose. Half-conscious, I realized that my right hand hurt but I couldn't look over to see why. Lundy was holding my head still and I couldn't holler because the doctor had my tongue. Finally, when I had a chance to look, a photographer was standing on my hand, to get a better angle for his picture. He got shooed away but then I heard them talking about getting a stretcher to take me to the ambulance. I could talk by now.

"No stretcher," I said. "You're not going to put me on a stretcher like a dead man. I walked in. I'll walk out."

I meant it. I've always been buggy about stretchers. They backed up the ambulance down behind the bench and I climbed in. I didn't lay down, either. I sat up in there. For the next couple days at Mercy Hospital, I was in and out of a daze. Like when Pam visited me, I'd be talking to her and then I'd look away. But when I looked back to tell her something, she'd be gone. I'd ring for the nurse.

"Where'd my wife go?" I'd ask her.

"She left two hours ago," she'd say.

I thought she'd been gone a few seconds. That's what a concussion does to you. I was conscious for a while, but then I was unconscious for I don't know how long. One time Dr. Virgin came in and started to explain what was wrong with me. I listened for a few seconds, but then I began to feel tired and I put my head on my pillow. The next thing I knew, he was gone.

I thought everybody was playing tricks on me.

Another time I got up to look around. I glanced in the mirror and scared myself. I looked like Frankenstein—my eyes were black-and-blue, purple really, and in my right eye there was no white. It was all a burgundy color. It looked like a little glass of wine. I really was an evil-looking thing.

I wanted to play the next Sunday, but they wouldn't let me. The game after that, I got knocked out again but not as bad. The next game, I had headaches again.

That's when the Dolphins got me a water helmet. Inside, it had a network of pads with tiny canals that were supposed to absorb the shock. I wore it the rest of that season. But in an exhibition game my second year, I caught a pass and turned and ran into a linebacker. My facemask went under his, burst his lips and knocked out a couple of his teeth. His facemask came over the top of mine and hit me across the nose. My nose was really splattered. I don't know if it affected my eardrum or if the blood got into the ear, but I really had a raw ear. I hardly slept for a week.

Bill Braucher of the Miami *Herald* wrote a story with the headline: "Injuries May End Csonka's Career." He's a good reporter and he quoted several people as being concerned about my future. In another story, an unidentified Miami neurosurgeon was quoted as saying: "If this sort of thing keeps up, Larry Csonka would be compelled to reevaluate his occupation."

But it didn't keep up. As soon as I felt better, I discarded the water helmet. I've never had any more problems. My rookie year, some of the coaches blamed my concussion on the way I carried the ball with both hands because, they said, "Zonk likes to hit people with his head." Which was

NOBODY EVER SAYS HE'S SORRY | 71

bullshit right there. I don't lower my head. I don't dive
and land on my head. It was just a freak way that I was
tackled. I've been tackled the same way a few times since
then with no repercussions. Or concussions.

I've kept a clipping of that story. Other people apparently thought my career was in jeopardy. But quitting never
entered my mind. I like to say that my headaches went
away when my blocking got better.

I've always considered pain to be as much a part of
football as my uniform. As a kid, I realized right away that
pain had to be part of it. I just tried to dish out more than
I got. That stems from my family. On a farm, somebody is
always smashing a thumb or putting a nail through their
foot. Things like that happened all the time.

To stand around and cry and moan was a waste of
time. My dad and mom wouldn't put up with it.

My mom would clean it, slap a Band-Aid on it, and
tell me to get out the door and do whatever I had been
doing. That's the way it was. I assumed that's the way it
was with everybody. Like at Syracuse, when I saw guys in
agony over little things like having an ingrown toenail cut
out, I couldn't believe it. I thought, Those guys are sissies.

*I was the same way. As kids, we played football with
no equipment. If you got kneed in the thigh, it was easy to
quit. Some guys did, but I never did. I always wanted to play.*

That's the way it is with my little boys, Doug and Paul,
because Pam treats them the same way my mom treated
me. The younger one, Paul, has nobody else his age to play
with, so he has to play with Doug and the other boys two
or three years older. When he gets his hands on the football, he has to make it count. One time, he was running,
looking back, when he ran smack into the side of the house.
He took a gouge out of the skin above and below the eye.

He came into the house screaming but Pam got him

quiet. She put some ice on it, then a Band-Aid, and he was out playing again.

If she had looked at him and said, "Oh, my God, you poor child," he would've opened his mouth like Grand Canyon, but she knew how to handle him. She didn't get excited so he didn't get excited. When the older one gets scratched like that, he doesn't even come into the house anymore. He gave up on us sympathizing with him.

I was never babied as a kid, but Alice grew up without any men around. When something happens to Brandon, she runs to him.

"He's all right," I always tell her. "Forget it. He'll be all right. Don't make a big fuss. He's got to learn to take it."

She thinks I'm cruel, but when she runs over he'll start crying more. When she's out and I'm watching him, if something happens I just ignore it. He'll look at me and figure everything must be all right. I don't mean with serious things, but with little bumps and scrapes it's ridiculous to make a big fuss about it.

Brandon's my godson, and when he was just toddling he liked to crawl up on an end table and dive headfirst into a bean-bag chair. That just amazed me. My kids were like that but I never noticed anybody else's kids do that. So when Brandon did it, I thought that was the greatest thing since crab apples.

If you baby kids, they'll always be babies.

One day when Pam was playing tennis, Doug nicked his forehead in the playground. He came over crying, but Pam told him: "Take my handkerchief out of my purse and put it on your head until I finish this set."

She's the perfect mother for my children.

5

Lincoln Park

My father, George Kiick, was a running back in the NFL with the Pittsburgh Steelers. He made $175 a game in 1940, and $200 a game in 1945. In between, he was a lieutenant in the Army in World War II. I've heard that in Africa or Italy he saved his whole platoon and got the Silver Star for it. Once when I was little, I asked him about it and he told me: "Ask your mother."

I never did. But it wasn't unusual for my father not to talk about his Army career because he doesn't talk much about anything. He's the strong silent type. Out in Lincoln Park, a few miles west of Paterson, about half an hour now from the George Washington Bridge on Route 80, he's known as "Big George." He's a solid six feet, about 210, still in good shape.

Big George doesn't say much but he's got that look. He's got a nice smile, except that he doesn't smile much.

He didn't yell at me much when I was little, either. But one time when I was a sophomore in high school, I was

beating on my little brother Bill and he came downstairs
and gave me a backhand that sent me flying across the table.
He had been a great athlete at Bucknell, where my mother
met him. He works for Rheingold beer now in its Orange,
New Jersey, plant. My mother Alice is a first-grade teacher
at the Pine Brook school. My father never pushed me into
sports. But once he saw that I enjoyed sports, he tried to
help me. Like when I was little, there always was a football
or a basketball or a baseball glove for me under the Christmas tree. The kids in the neighborhood depended on me
to supply some kind of ball. One time I brought a new
basketball down to the playground, but the older guys
grabbed it.

"Hey, that's my ball," I said.

"Don't worry, we'll choose you."

But when they chose up sides, I was left sitting there
while they used my ball. Not that I argued. I got to play a
lot for a little kid. And my father helped me. Especially in
football. At first I thought he was too critical. Like if I
made some good runs, he'd hardly mention them. But he'd
tell me about the block I missed. At first it bothered me
because it seemed like he was never satisfied. But then I
realized that he was trying to help me, to make me a better
player, to make me work harder. I knew that when I came
home, I'd hear what I did wrong.

His criticism really helped me because it was construc-
tive. I tried to improve so he wouldn't have anything to
criticize.

I haven't changed that much from when I was a kid.
I started dreaming about playing in the NFL when I was
ten years old. That was 1956 when the New York Giants
won the NFL title, when pro football really began to get
big. Living near New York, the Giants were our team. My
uncle, Dr. Kurt Manrodt, had season tickets and sometimes

I'd go to a game with him. I was a big Frank Gifford fan.
But mostly I'd watch the road games on TV and listen to
the home games on radio. Just from the excitement of it,
at half time me and my brother would go outside into the
backyard to play football. He was five years younger than I
was, and he made me think I was a good football player.
I figured I must be good if I could run over my little brother.

I should hope you could run over him.

That's the truth. It never occurred to me that I was
running over him because he was five years younger. I just
thought that if I was doing it, I must be a good football
player. In our games, he was always the underdog.

I should think he'd be the underdog.

My biggest heartbreak as a kid was listening to the
sudden-death overtime game in 1958 when the Giants lost
to the Colts for the NFL championship. I almost cried. In
our games in the backyard, I always pretended to be Frank
Gifford, or Billy Cannon of LSU because LSU was the big
college team then. Against my brother, I could score anytime I wanted. I'd hold the score to like 7–7, but when
there were ten seconds left I'd break loose to win. My
brother got so frustrated. We had three fields in the backyard. The best grass was where we pretended to be the pro
teams, the next best was for the college games and the worst
part was where we played what we called our "dirty football"
games. In those "dirty" games, one of us always was the
Chicago Bears.

The time I visited Lincoln Park, I didn't see enough
room in your backyard for three fields.

You're thinking of the house where we live now. But
when I was little, we lived with my grandparents, Fred and

Elfreda Lohr, my mother's parents, a few blocks away in a little stone house with a fireplace and a low roof. George Washington is supposed to have slept in that house during the Revolutionary War, that's how old it is.

It's real tiny. I wasn't ten feet inside it when I hit my head on a beam, but Jim's grandparents fit the house because they're tiny people. Jim's grandfather is the most complete man I've ever met.

He writes music. He makes his own furniture. Anything that's broken, he can fix it. He did all my high school projects for me. He didn't want to, but I coaxed him into doing them. I was very dumb in physics and the teacher knew it. The teacher couldn't understand how I came in with this project that measured the intensity of candlelight. My grandfather had made it with a candle at one end and a light bulb at the other. It was brilliant. I got an A on it.

Your grandfather got an A on it.

My grandfather didn't like to be corrected if he knew he was right. In my algebra homework one night, he showed me how to solve a problem easier and faster than the teacher's way. The next day the teacher told me: "Your answer is correct but your method is incorrect."

That night, when I told my grandfather, he searched through the algebra book for mistakes—any kind, grammatical, typographical. He sent me back to the teacher the next day with the mistakes circled. And he was always fixing my bicycle. Before he retired, he appraised machinery. But he wasn't just smart with machines. He knew everything. We used to take the dictionary, pick out a word, and ask him what it meant. He knew them all. He's eighty-two now, but he mows his own lawn. He's probably in better shape than I am.

My grandmother was an actress in vaudeville. She's still a beautiful lady. Our whole family lived with them until I was about thirteen. By that time I was really playing football.

Lincoln Park had a Lower End, down by the Passaic River, and an Upper End, where we lived. We used to beat the Lower End all the time because myself and Roy Ferrara were bigger than everybody else. We played on the dirt field at the Lincoln Park grammar school and I really thought I could play then, because I was fast. I don't know what happened to my speed but I was very fast then. On that dirt field I was fantastic. Then one day a man named Lenny Familio talked with us about starting a team.

"We'll get uniforms," he told us.

We were all for that, so we accepted him as the coach. We had one kid who was terrible, but his old man owned the Shoprite supermarket and he bought our uniforms. They were blue and gold with stars all over them. They were beautiful. We had helmets, too. But the team was made up of kids from both the Lower End and the Upper End, and now we had nobody to play against.

If you had lived in Stow, Ohio, you'd have had some competition. You'd have had to fight to keep those uniforms and helmets.

We finally got some games but we always got killed. I didn't play much. I was behind Charley Albano—he's a jockey now, that's how big we were. He rides at the Miami tracks. I see him sometimes. But then somebody got hurt and they made me the quarterback. All I ran was the option. I was the first Wishbone quarterback. I either pitched it or ran. One game over in West Paterson we lost like 32–0, and afterwards Lenny Familio thought he was Vince Lombardi.

"I'm going to make you kids walk home," he said.

It was a good five miles. And he really meant it. But some of the parents talked him out of it. That team in West Paterson had been playing together like five years. No wonder they killed us. But the experience of playing organized football really helped me. By the time I was in Boonton High School, I only weighed a hundred pounds but I made the freshman team. I didn't play much, only at the end of the game and mostly as a defensive back, once in a while as a running back. But even then I was very conscious of the way I dressed in football. Nobody on the freshman team wore lowcuts but I rolled my socks down over my hightops. Everybody thought I had lowcuts, like the pros. Frank Gifford was wearing them on the Giants then, and I thought I looked as cool as him.

My freshman year, the school paper had a feature on what you wanted to be when you grew up. I put "Pro football player." From the harassment I got from the other kids, you'd have thought I wanted to be the President, but I didn't consider it that far out. I just knew what I wanted to be.

But all through high school, I always had trouble with coaches. Not my football coach, Joe Molitoris; he was great. But things kept happening to me with the other coaches. My freshman baseball coach, Kieffer Shriner, was an elderly man, a very well-known coach in New Jersey, but very set in his ways. He really dug the rah-rah type of player and I wasn't his type. One day he looked at my shortstop's mitt. It wasn't an expensive mitt but it was molded to my hand. It fit perfect but it looked worn out.

"You need a new mitt," he said. "I'll bring one tomorrow."

"No, Coach," I said. "This mitt is fine. I love this mitt."

But the next day, he brought a new mitt. It must've cost thirty dollars but it was flat and hard. I couldn't catch anything with it. When we went out to take infield, I changed to my old mitt. When he noticed it, he came over to me.

"Where's your new mitt?" he said.

"I can't use it, Coach," I said.

"Go home," he said. "Go home now."

I didn't practice that day but the next day I wore my old mitt again. He didn't say anything but all I ever heard from him after that was how I had a bad attitude. Another time we took a bus to play Morris Catholic in baseball. When we got there, I realized I had forgotten my baseball cap. He spotted me right away.

"Where's your cap?" he said.

"I don't know, Coach. I guess I left it back at school."

"Get back on the bus," he said.

I sat on the bus the whole game. He didn't want to, but he really did me a favor. It was one of those cold spring days, really cold. I always hated to play baseball when it was cold. Your hands sting from hitting the ball in the cold. But that day I stayed warm on the bus while everybody froze. My sophomore year, a similar thing happened. The coach told me and the catcher, Al Venturini, who was the quarterback on the football team, to run a few laps. Punishment for something.

"My asthma's bothering me," I said. "I can't do it."

I walked off and that was the last time I played baseball. Al Venturini, too. The football coach, Joe Molitoris, wanted us to change our mind.

"I'm sorry," I told him. "It's not worth the aggravation."

In basketball the coach, Glenn Moore, was a very religious man, very straight. One time during a game, a guy elbowed me and I elbowed him back. But when I came over to the bench, the coach told me: "Don't ever do that again.

If somebody elbows you, go to the official and say, 'Mr. Official, number sixteen is giving me the elbow.' "

To me, talking to the official wasn't the way to solve it. But the coach always preferred to do things formally. Near the end of the football season my junior year, I had a cyst at the base of my spine. It broke in one game and there was blood seeping through my pants. I guess it looked awful but it didn't hurt that much. It had hurt more before the cyst broke, before the pressure was released. I needed an operation to remove it completely. After the operation I wanted to start playing basketball, so I went to Dr. Forrest Chilton, my mother's uncle. He told me I could play but Glenn Moore told me: "You need a note from the doctor who did the operation."

I argued that Dr. Chilton had assisted on the operation, what difference did it make. But the coach said: "What are you trying to do, hurt the team?"

Then the school nurse claimed my parents were pushing me into playing basketball, but all I wanted to do was play basketball. I always thought coaches liked the kids who wanted to play no matter what.

Another time Glenn Moore brought Al Venturini and myself into his office.

"You two are hanging around too much," he said. "You're hurting morale."

We were good friends but we got along with everybody else. After practice, we liked to shoot fouls together. Big deal. I couldn't understand how that was hurting morale on the team. Then after his talk, we came out and shot foul shots together anyway. That really pissed him off. But he was just that kind of coach. It seems like I ran into that type coach quite often. I'm beginning to think it's me, but I don't really have a bad attitude. Sometimes it might look

*that way. I do things lazily. I guess I look like I've got a
bad attitude.*

His eyes are always half closed, that's Jim's problem.

*People always thought it was me. Like the baseball
coach I had trouble with, Kieffer Shriner, was my health
teacher, too. I had got A's the first semester. It was impossible for me to fail. Impossible. But one day this kid Jim
Docherty organized a laugh-in. At three o'clock everybody
in the health class would start laughing. But unfortunately
for me, about ten of three the teacher kicked me out of the
classroom. I forget what the reason was, but I had to stand
in the hall. And at three o'clock, I was out there when
everybody started laughing.*

*Naturally the teacher thought I had been the insti-
gator. He came out and told me to write a paper on manners.*

*I went home and wrote a ridiculous paper. I wrote
things like "Mickey Mantle has manners" and "Sandy
Koufax has manners," and when I turned it in the next day
he refused to accept it. He gave me an incomplete in the
course. My mother really got after him. She wrote a paper
for me that was fantastic. At the end of it, she wrote how
the teacher is responsible for a student's motivation, too.
I got by the course but it was another ridiculous thing that
I was in the middle of.*

*At my graduation, all those ridiculous things cost me
being voted the best athlete in my class.*

*Not winning that trophy has bothered me ever since.
The kid they gave it to was a good athlete. He ran track and
cross-country. His name was Gerry Dorer and we were good
friends. But there was no doubt in everybody's mind that I
was the best all-around athlete. After they announced it at
graduation, he told me: "You deserved it, Jim."*

I appreciated that because he didn't have to say it. I found out later that the coaches I'd had trouble with had voted against me. Kieffer Shriner, Glenn Moore. Even the student president of the Varsity Club didn't like me. His name was Ron Wild. He was a running back, too. We were co-captains. We once were good friends but we got to like different things. I liked to drink and fool around but he didn't get into that. So he criticized me. I told him: "It's none of your business what I do."

One day I showed up at a Varsity Club meeting needing a shave and with a sweater over my T-shirt. He gave me a big lecture.

"Shove the Varsity Club up your ass," I told him.

After that, the conflict between us got worse and worse. One day we started to scuffle.

"You won't hit me," he said.

I really went after him, but our phys ed teacher, Tom Pagani, grabbed me. Tom Pagani was a hammer thrower, 6-5 and 250. He just picked me up and held me. Ever since then, Ron Wild really has tried to be buddies with me.

I lost that trophy in high school, too. The guy that beat me out was a golfer. That really pissed me off. I liked the guy. Ron Houser, a nice guy. But when they gave the award, they made it sound like he was more of an athlete than he was. It really bugged me. A golfer.

But that baseball coach, Kieffer Shriner, really did me a favor. Without him knowing it. Without him wanting to.

I had quit his baseball team, so he kept telling everybody, "Jim Kiick is a quitter, he'll never make it." That stuck in my mind. My freshman year at Wyoming, many times I felt like leaving and going home. But then I'd remember what that man said. I was determined to prove him wrong. Even when I was a rookie with the Dolphins, there were times I felt like going home. But the same thing would pop into my mind. I've got to give that man some credit for my success.

But in my high school years, if I didn't like something, I just didn't do it.

Like my summer jobs; I never was much of a worker. One time when I really needed some money for something, I went over to the Knoll Country Club in Boonton to caddy. I'd never caddied before. I didn't realize I had to sit around the caddy yard until I was called. I didn't like that and I didn't take to the caddy master, either. He was a real rough guy. After about three hours, he finally looked at me.

"You ever caddy before?" he said.

"Yeah, about three years," I lied.

"Double for these ladies," he said.

I walked over to where the two ladies' golf bags were, like I'd been doing it all my life. But then I picked up the bags the wrong way. Upside down. All the clubs bounced out in a big clatter. And the caddy master started yelling.

"Goodbye," I told him.

I didn't need his aggravation. I just left on the spot. Another time I was working for the road department, but the boss didn't like me because I wasn't old enough to drive. In the morning, he'd say: "Sam, take that truck. Joe, you take the other truck. Kid, you . . . you go with Joe. Damn it, kid, I wish you could drive."

One day I was sickling weeds around a stop sign. I sickled with my right hand so I had my left hand in my pocket. I guess I looked too relaxed for the boss when he came driving up to check on us.

"Kid," he yelled, "you got to put more into it."

I couldn't figure out what was bothering him. Hell, I was doing my job sickling the weeds.

"Kid," he yelled, "take your hand out of your pocket."
I finished the day's work but that was all. I didn't need his aggravation either.

You just had a bad attitude.

The best job I ever had was the summer after I graduated from high school. I was a meter reader; you know, go from house to house to read the gas and electric meters in the cellar. I'd ring the bell and yell, "Your meter reader's here." In the morning, some ladies would answer the door in their negligee.

Get the hat, get the hat.

I swear to God they did.

How many times did you ever have a chick in a negligee answer the door?

All the time, Zonk, honest.

Not even with a bathrobe on?

Some would have a bathrobe on. Some would just have a negligee on, a nightgown.

In Stow, Ohio, chicks do not answer the door with a nightgown on.

This wasn't Stow, Ohio, this was New Jersey where things are really advanced.

In Stow, Ohio, when I was collecting for newspapers, fat old ladies answered the door not only fully clothed but with their dogs snapping at my heels. Those dogs really had me jumping around. I never saw a chick in a negligee.

How old were you?

I was about fourteen.

I was going into college. It's different. If you were a meter reader, you'd know. You've heard about the milkman stories, but a meter reader is in the house. I was right inside the house. I can't go into details.

You ever score?

Yeah, sure I did.

You're shittin' me?

It was a good job. I was on my own. I had this little book that I wrote down the meter numbers in. If there was a mean dog at a house, I'd estimate the meter and keep going. But it was a good job. Some people even gave you lunch.

Lunch wasn't what you were looking for. "Let me see your meter." How many times did you score?

I don't remember. I really don't remember.

Don't you dare tell me that you lost track.

I didn't mark them down. It didn't happen every day. It wasn't an everyday thing.

Let me tell you something. If I was a meter reader, especially if I was that young, I definitely would remember how many times, who, where they lived. I'd remember all of it.

That was a long time ago.

You're telling some big lies in your old age.

Three times. You happy now?

Blondes, brunettes or redheads.

That was a good job. I kept that job all summer until

I went to college. But except for playing pro football, I've never had a real job that I've had to go to every day. Like in the off-season, my wife Alice wants me to get a job and I'll go out in the morning. But then I'll play basketball for a while and have a few beers, then come home and tell her, "Nothing today, honey." That's the way I go through life. Just having a good time. Like the guys I grew up with in Lincoln Park, they just have a good time. Some work. Some don't. But they're all having a good time.

Which ones work?

Kenny McCaffrey works. He's got a job.

Kenny didn't work the week I was there.

You were in town. That was a big event.

Nobody worked.

Kenny, Steve Gerrisch, Al Eckelkamp, Ron Rensing, and Richie Terpstra, they all took off so we could play basketball.

They each said, "Oh, I called in today . . ."

They're thirty-five-year-old kids. I know I'm going to be the same way. I mean, they work. Sometimes. But they're fantastic guys. They're just crazy about sports. Like our rookie year, we were in New York to play the Jets and I asked Zonk if he wanted to go out to my hometown the night before the game.

We had to be back by eleven, but sometimes George Wilson didn't check. It was a gamble but we decided to go.

After the workout at Shea Stadium, we went to the Port Authority terminal near Times Square to hop a bus.

This was a big adventure for me. I'd been in New York

a few times but I'd never gone from the city to New Jersey on a bus. What a crazy place that Port Authority terminal is. I don't know how anybody finds their bus. We were upstairs where the platforms are, looking all over. We found one bus sitting there, but Jim didn't know if it was our bus or not. Nobody knows. You just get on one and take a chance.

I always get lost when I go there. I used to park my car in the lot on the roof of the bus terminal when I drove into the city, then I'd get on the elevator and go down to the street. I pretty well knew where I was. But looking for a bus, I didn't know where I was. I'd never taken the bus much. I didn't know where the platform was. We were roaming around, looking for it. We finally found it.

Jim was taking me, but I knew as much about it as he did.

We got home for dinner. My mother cooked ravioli for us. Afterwards me and Zonk went to Henny's, the local bar. It's really Henri's, but in Lincoln Park not many people are that sophisticated so we call it Henny's. It's a great place. And that night, it was packed. All the guys were there.

It was one of the greatest nights I've ever had.

We didn't particularly want to drink. We had a game the next day. But all the guys were buying us drinks. Jack Daniel's and water, that's what we drink all the time.

First drink I ever bought Jim was a Jack Daniel's and water when we met at the College All-Star game. He's never changed.

That night in Henny's the NFL Highlights came on television. All of a sudden, the TV voice mentions me and Zonk, and a big cheer went up. All the guys yelled and screamed, "Yay . . . Yay." Here we were drinking with them and now we're on TV too in the same bar. They really enjoyed it. They weren't making a big fuss over us or anything. We didn't want them to do that. We just wanted them to treat us like regular guys.

I didn't want to come back to the hotel. I wanted to stay there all night. Have a few drinks and shoot some pool. What a great bar.

That's just the way these guys are. They're really avid sports fans. They know everything that's going on in sports. They know all the statistics. And they still love to play sports. You can always get a basketball game going. They like to bet maybe five dollars a game, whatever. They play everything in season. Basketball. Softball. Football. Not touch football either. They play tackle with no equipment, no helmet, nothing. After my rookie year, when I went home for a couple weeks like I always do after the season, the guys had a big game coming up against one of the neighboring towns.

"We hate to ask for a favor," one of them said, "but Saturday we've got this big game. They beat us the last two weeks."

"I really shouldn't do it," I said. "Like if I got hurt, I'd really be in trouble with the Dolphins . . . Oh, what the hell."

My mother went nuts when she found out I was going to play. No equipment, nothing. But fortunately it really rained that day. It was really muddy. Nobody ever gets hurt much in the mud. I wore a sweatshirt and jeans. After the game I was so muddy they wouldn't let me in the car. But the big thing was, we won. I threw a touchdown pass to my brother. You hear that, Zonk, I threw a touchdown pass.

I heard you, but I don't believe you.

We got some great guys in Lincoln Park; like Richie Terpstra, he thinks he's a great defensive end. He's got hair all over. We call him "Filthy McNasty." But he's a helluva guy. Deep inside he knows he really couldn't play in the NFL, but he likes to bullshit about it. Like the night I brought Zonk into Henny's, he came over to me.

"I could tackle you and Larry, one on one," he said.

"Me, maybe you could," I said. "Because I wouldn't try to run over you after I faked you. But there's no way you could tackle Zonk one on one. He'd kill you."

"The hell he would," Richie said.

But a couple hours later, after a few more drinks, he came over to me and whispered: "The more I look at Zonk, the more I think you're right."

After the 1971 season, there was a big testimonial banquet for me at the Wayne Manor, a few miles away. All the guys were there. I wanted to wear a tux, just for laughs, but I knew a tux would've been too much for Lincoln Park, especially with me wearing it. They wouldn't have been able to handle that. I got driven over in a limousine. Really classy. After the whole thing was over, I came out looking for the limousine again. But they'd rented it just for the ride over, not for the ride home. I had to pile into another car.

Going over, Jim didn't have enough room for me in the limousine. I rode in the cop's car that was leading us.

The cop driving that car was Ron Wild, the guy I had the fight with in high school after I didn't shave for the Varsity Club meeting.

He was talking about Jim like they were old buddies. He sounded like he was Jim's biggest fan now.

6

Stow

I was a Christmas baby in Stow, Ohio, but when my birthday came around each year, I really never thought about it
as my birthday. Christmas was a big holiday at our house.
Csonka is a Hungarian name and on Christmas all our
Hungarian relatives from Akron to Kent came to our farm.
My father had homemade wine, my mother had all kinds
of food. The festivities lasted from Christmas to New Year's,
the whole week. It was great. Years later, somebody asked
me if I got an extra present on Christmas for my birthday
but I never did. It never even occurred to me to expect an
extra present.

I'd be pissed off if I didn't get an extra present.

I didn't mind because I always had such a great time.
Our farmhouse was on about thirty acres with trees and
woods and a pasture for our beefstock. Nothing fancy. But
nothing was fancy in my family. I was baptized Larry Rich-
ard Csonka, not Lawrence like you might expect. Our

farmhouse was the same way. My father built it out of cement blocks.

When all my cousins came out to visit us at Christmas, we had the sled runs ready. Some were maybe two hundred feet long, with straight drops in spots. We'd build snow-banks on the hills, then spray water over them with a hose until they were so icy that you literally could skate on them.

You were at the mercy of where the ice took you. If the ice took you toward a tree, you hit the tree.

One time we had this old sled we had nailed back together. It was about eight feet long. I was on the back. I thought I'd be safe there. But we hit this big ol' maple, full tilt. When the sled bucked forward, I sailed off the back into the tree, face first. My nose started bleeding. One of the local kids, Billy Goykoff, had on a white coat he just got for Christmas and he was yelling, "Don't bleed on my coat!"

I couldn't help it. I was bleeding all over everybody and he was crying and screaming. He got up with blood all over his new white coat and he ran all the way home.

Your nose is always bleeding.

Except that I didn't run home, he did. But when I was a kid, I was always bleeding. One time I jumped out of a barn and landed on a board with a nail on it. The nail came up through the top of my shoe. I thought I'd missed it until I went to pull my foot up. Then when I put my other foot on the board, I stepped on another nail that went into my arch. Talk about hurt.

I had to ride my bike over three miles to get home. By the time I got there, my shoe was full of blood.

"I'll fix that up," my dad said. "I'll put some sliced tomatoes on it overnight to draw out the wound."

That was one of my dad's home cures. Except that it

didn't work. My foot got infected instead. My dad thought that tomatoes were a cure for almost anything. My dad, Joe Csonka, and my mom, Mildred, had their hands full with six kids—Joe, Norita, Anita, me, Nancy, and Andy. My mom is like Jim's mom, a very nice person, a real mom. She put up with a lot with me. Like when I was about fifteen, I had a set of 110-pound weights. I didn't have any place to do a bench press so I'd lay on my bed and do it. Afterwards, I'd just leave the weights there. She'd come up to make the bed but she couldn't pick up even one end of them. She'd have to call my dad and he'd get mad, but she never did. Now that she's got more time to herself with most of the kids grown up, she delivers mail. I come from tough stock. She likes to tell people that when I was really little, I'd bring in flowers from the woods for her and say to her: "Ain't me nice."

My brother Joe didn't think I was so nice. I was always trying to get into whatever he was doing. I don't remember this, but my mom tells me that my brother used to tie me to trees or put big rocks in my diaper to slow me down. I loved animals, too. All kinds. Once when I was really little, about five, our dogs had a tomcat cornered under a brush pile. We had some wild border collies then, really strong dogs. They were literally killing this cat. I've always had a tremendous compassion for animals, and when I heard the cat screeching I ran out of the house and dove into the brush pile.

I grabbed the cat by the neck and tried to pull it out. But the cat, not knowing any better, turned on me and bit me right through the knuckles behind the index finger of my right hand. I've still got the scar.

My brother Joe grabbed me by the feet and dragged me out backwards. But the cat hung on my hand for a couple seconds, then it leaped away. The dogs jumped on it and did kill it then, but I was screaming from the pain of the bite. My hand was all blood. My dad worked nights so he slept days. All the barking and screeching and screaming had woken him up. When he was sleeping days, he did not like waking up to screaming children.

He came running out of the house, with just his pants on. I stopped crying and held up my hand so he could see the blood. Otherwise he would've whacked me before I could explain it.

He took me inside and poured green soap on my hand. Hospital green soap that really stung. I didn't say a word. You didn't scream around my father. If you did, he hit you. In those days he was really hypertense. He was working nights in the Goodyear plant in Akron and he had a TV-repair shop going in the daytime. So he didn't get much sleep.

In those years, my mother woke him up with the tip of a broom handle. She'd just touch him and he'd be on his feet looking at her. I thought everybody's father woke up that way.

When my dad got mad, look out. When he was young, growing up in Akron, he was a bouncer in a movie theater in Goosetown, a ghetto where the Hungarians and the blacks lived. The theater was known as Joe's Boxing Arena because my dad put on the best show. Guys paid ten cents to go to the movies just to try boxing with him. Every weekend he had two or three good brawls. He's not too big, just under six feet, but he's husky. He never got beat. One time he hit a guy so hard with his right hand, the guy went backwards through a window and hit his head on the curbstone. My dad had a tremendous right hand.

When he got taken to court by that guy he put through the window, the judge told my dad that from then on there would be a ban on his fists, that they would be

considered lethal weapons, just like they are with professional boxers.

It's too bad my dad never had any training as a boxer.
He really had an instinct for it. But he was too busy trying
to make a living. The judge's ban finished him as a bouncer.
He went to work for Goodyear and moved the family out
into the country. It was safer for him out there because the
judge had warned him: "The next time you're up on any
kind of a charge for using your hands, you're going to jail."

After that, every time my dad got into a fight, my mom
got scared as hell. But that didn't stop my dad from using
his hands if he thought he was justified. One time when
I was small we had an insurance man, a pudgy red-haired
smart-ass, who had sold my dad a policy. One day he was
at our house giving my mom a bad time about us being
behind in the payments. He even was making me mad, the
way he was acting. He thought my dad was at work but
my dad was upstairs sleeping.

"You better talk quieter," my mom told him, "or my
husband will hear you."

But my dad already had heard him. In our house, then,
we didn't have a staircase up to where the bedrooms were.
It was just a ladder up to a loft. I heard Dad's feet hit the
floor upstairs. Two seconds later, he hit the bottom of the
landing in one jump. When the red-haired guy saw him,
he started backing up, waving his hands, trying to talk. But
my dad grabbed him and they both went through the
screen door.

My dad was careful. He never did hit him with his
fists. He just cuffed him. Then he stuffed him in his car,
ripped up the insurance policy, and threw it at him. That
little guy was so shook up, he drove off right across the lawn.

Another time we were out delivering a TV set in our
little Rambler, driving along a narrow country road, when

a big Buick came roaring up behind us. My dad saw him coming and pulled over to the right as far as he could. Driving the Buick was a guy in a suit and hat, with a big pot belly, a businessman. As he got alongside us, he yelled: "Good thing you pulled over or I'd have blown that Rambler off the road."

My dad didn't say a word but his neck turned red. When his neck turned red, that was the sign. Instead of delivering the TV set, he caught up to the Buick, passed it real easy, got about a mile ahead, and parked crosswise, blocking the road. Then he got out and waited. When the Buick arrived, the businessman rolled down his window and yelled at my dad. That was his second mistake. My dad reached in, half pulled him out the window and slapped the hell out of him.

"Now," my dad said, "what was it you wanted to say?"

The one incident I remember best involved an auto accident my brother Joe had. He was stopped for a red light when another guy bumped into him from the back. There wasn't any damage to speak of, just a couple scratches. My brother told him to forget it. But the guy told the police that my brother had backed into him. He even was going to sue my brother. He came to the house a few times when my dad was working and he got a little loud with my mom.

"You better go away," she told him, "before my husband comes home."

"I'm not scared of your husband," he growled. "I'm not scared of him."

He kept talking, so my mom shut the door in his face. When my dad got home, my mom told him about it and I could see his neck turn red. The next Saturday, my dad and I were coming back from picking strawberries when I saw the guy talking to my mom. I took a quick look at my dad and his neck was really red. I just knew that this guy's ass was grass now. He was a big dude, too, in pretty good shape. But he made a bad mistake. When they started arguing, he pointed a finger in my dad's face.

My dad hit him a right hand, and spit and snot just flew. Some of the guy's teeth caved in and he fell back across the hood of his car.

But the guy had guts. He bounced off the car and threw a punch that caught my dad in the mouth. My dad had been smoking a little cigar. He hadn't even taken it out of his mouth when he hit the guy. So when the guy hit him, the lit end burned my dad's lip. Now he was really hot. He just ran over the top of the guy, grabbed him by the shirt, and hit him so many times the guy's head was flipping back and forth. By now, my mom was on my dad's back, trying to hold him.

The guy was crying now, sobbing like a little kid. My dad stepped back.

The guy got into his car. But then he made another mistake. He mumbled something under his breath. I don't know what he said, but I do know that you just don't say certain words to my dad in front of my mother. Whatever the guy said, my dad really snapped. The guy had his car moving but my dad pulled him part way out of the window and really splattered him with a right hand in the nose. Blood flew across the windshield. Then my dad stuffed him back in the car. As the guy drove off, my dad kicked the car a couple times.

Sure enough, just as my mom feared, the Stow police came out to the house. They knew Dad and they weren't about to get him riled up. You couldn't imagine nicer fellows. They even made sure not to have their guns with them. When they came into the house, they sat and talked very nicely.

"Joe," the police chief said quietly, "let's sit down and have a drink."

My mom put out a big bottle of bourbon and some glasses for everybody.

"Joe," the police chief finally said, "I'm going to have to take you in."

But my dad talked him out of having to go to the station house. The chief brought the papers out to our house and my dad signed them. The day the case went to court, the other guy never showed up, so that was the end of that.

I've got a bad temper but I'm not as fast-tempered as my dad. He put up with a lot from me. I was the world's number-one dumb Hunky kid. Before he went to work early one morning, he woke me up, but I was still really asleep.

"Hedgerow, clear out the hedgerow," I heard him say. "Poplar trees. White cloths."

I went back to sleep. Later on, when I went to do the job, I cleared out the hedgerow. I also saw white cloths on a row of poplar trees that my dad loved. I cut down the poplars, quartered them, did a great job. Just as I finished, he came driving down the road. But he quickly slowed down.

"You weren't supposed to cut down those poplars," he exploded. "That's why I tied the white cloths around them. I told you that this morning."

Half asleep, I hadn't really understood what he wanted done. My dad was really pissed off. He really hollered. That was good in a way. When my dad hollered, you were all right. But when he grabbed you, you were in trouble. If you were going to get a thrashing, you didn't get a lecture first.

The only time he gave me a licking, and told me that

he was going to, was when I broke into a little cottage nearby with a friend of mine.

I don't know why we did. I knew the old couple who lived there, real nice people. One day when they weren't home, I threw a big rock through a window, then we climbed in and rummaged around. I can't figure to this day why I did that. When the police came out to investigate, it was the only time I ever looked my dad in the eye and told him a lie.

"Did you break in that house?" the policeman asked me.

I knew that if I said yes, my dad would kill me right on the spot, so I did the only thing to preserve my life.

"No, sir," I said, looking at my dad.

"That's it," my dad said. "He said no."

But then my accomplice admitted that we had done it. My heart sank.

"Go in the garage," Dad said. "And wait."

I thought about running away for a couple days until he cooled off but he read my mind.

"If you run," he said, "you'll still have to come back."

After the police left, he came into the garage with half an oak tree in his hand. I howled the first ten minutes, then I stopped for ten minutes, figuring if I kept my mouth shut maybe he'd stop. But then I gave up on that idea and went back to howling.

Not that my dad spent his life hitting people. He just never could take any shit, that's all.

He took me to my first football game to see my brother play. I was about nine and my brother was an end on the high school team. They played Friday nights. I didn't know that much about football. But in the first game I saw, my brother made a great catch. Everybody applauded. My dad took out a dollar bill and put it in my hand.

"Go down to the bench," he told me, "and tell Joe this is for making that great catch."

At the time, a dollar bill was like a fortune to me. And when I went down and gave it to Joe, he patted me on the head, he was real nice to me. Usually he didn't want anything to do with me. He was about sixteen then; his life was entirely different than mine. I was just a little kid. But standing down around the bench, I took it all in—the coach and the players, the uniforms, the crowd, the lights. It had an actual aroma, a combination of cigar smoke and the smell of hot dogs, popcorn, coffee, the whole thing. It was like a fantasy. And to be one of the players, that had to be the best part.

I knew right then that I was going to play football as soon as I could.

In the next few years, I played whenever I could. The summer before I went into the eighth grade, I gained thirty-five pounds and grew nearly three inches. All of a sudden I was one of the biggest kids in my class. The other kids in my class were still playing touch football but I was on the high school freshman team. I played center and middle guard. Just being able to play with guys a year older than me, I thought I had the world by the ass.

I kept growing, too. I was working on a dairy farm in those years. I guess that developed me. That and my dad's potions.

My dad was a nut on health food before it was popular. He was big on parsley. Organic iron, he called it. He'd go out in the garden and pick stuff that he thought was good for me. It might've been poison for all he knew but he'd pound it up and mix it with Geritol, which has a terrible taste. Then he'd put honey in it, so there was a sweet taste added to the terrible taste. It was awful.

"Drink it," he'd tell me.

Before every game, he made me drink half a pint of his concoction. I don't know if it fortified my body but it fortified my constitution. Just swallowing it, just knowing that I could cope with that stuff, made a better man out of me.

As a freshman in high school, I was on the junior varsity. I made the varsity as a sophomore. That was a real big deal.

I was a defensive end, and it was easy for me to excel because I was as big as the seniors were. My last game that season, I got to run with the ball. It was an accident. One of the guys on our short-kickoff team was hurt, so they put me in there. The kickoff bounced around to me and I took off with it. I ran over two tacklers before I realized what I was doing. I didn't score or save the game, but I got a tremendous feeling carrying the ball. I was thrashing around, trying to run six ways at once. I loved it. I knew then that I wanted to run with the ball. The next summer, when our team had its physical-fitness workouts, I always lined up with the running backs.

"You're a defensive end," the other players kept telling me. "You're too big and too slow to be a running back."

The other running backs kept giving me all kinds of grief but that just made me more determined. Before school opened, all the players who had lettered the year before went away on a camping trip for about six days to get to know each other. One day on that trip I had a few words with the other fullback, Ron Erving, and we had a pretty good brawl. I was choking him before the other guys realized what was happening and pulled me off.

That was when my coach, Dick Fortner, knew I meant it about wanting to be a running back.

The first game that season, I did real well and that was it. From then on, nobody told me I was too big or too slow. But at the time, I never thought about going to college or playing pro. I wanted to join the Merchant Marine. I'd read books about it and it really sounded great. I wanted to see the world.

But then I started going with Pam and she got me to answer the letters and questionnaires I was getting from colleges that wanted me as a football player.

I'm lucky I did. One of my best friends joined the Merchant Marine but he's out of it now. He discovered he spent more time looking at the ocean than he did in the exotic ports.

I grew up with some great kids and we had some great times. I hope they laugh about it now as much as I do. When most of us were around five feet tall, a kid named Teddy Augustyn was six feet. He stopped there. He's still six feet. He just grew up faster. He had big hands and big feet. And he was one of those kids who always wanted to be part of the gang. It took time but eventually we always could con him into doing almost anything. Like we had a big canvas baby buggy, with big whitewall rubber tires, that we used to ride down hills in. It was a great ride.

One day I got the idea to ride the baby buggy down the roof of a big barn on one of the nearby farms.

The roof was about sixty feet long on each side and it sloped up at the bottom. Next to one side was a chicken house with a flat-top roof. I had it all figured out. Ride the baby buggy down the side of the roof, then it will take the upslope and land on the chicken house. Everybody thought it was a great idea—especially me, because I was going to ride in the baby buggy. Except that when me and Teddy finally got it up on top of the roof, it looked a little steep to me.

"You take it down, Teddy," I said.

"Not me," he said. "It's all yours."

The other kids were hollering "C'mon, let's go," so I compromised.

"We'll both go, you get in first."

He hunched himself under the canvas top, with his big knees poking out.

"Get in," he said. "C'mon, get in."

I turned him loose. He was yelling "You son of a biiitttccchhh" as the baby buggy was going down the roof, kavoom, kavoom. It must've got up to sixty miles an hour in two seconds. But when it hit the upslope of the roof, it didn't turn up. The wheels and the undercarriage slammed into that upslope and stopped. The top part, the canvas bag where Teddy was, kept going. He went flying through the air, his big knees sticking out, but instead of landing on the chicken-house roof, he slammed into the side. It sounded like a bowling ball hitting a bunch of tenpins. Crunch, the canvas bag folded up, Teddy's legs quivered, and he went straight down in a heap.

I thought sure he had to be really hurt. But we untangled him and walked him around and he was all right.

Not two weeks later, one of the farmers had a big auction. Teddy and I pooled our funds, which meant maybe we had a dollar between us. We had bid up to fifty cents on everything just for fun. But when they put up an old grandfather's chair, we kept bidding and we got it. For eighty-five cents.

"Let's put it in our tree house," Teddy said.

It wasn't really a tree house. It was just a platform up in a big oak tree. But it was about two miles away. We spent all that afternoon lugging it over there. We'd carry it a little ways, then sit down and eat apples, then carry it another little ways. When we finally got it there, we used a rope to pull the chair up onto the platform, about forty feet up.

"Let's take turns sitting in it," I said.

After a couple minutes, I got off the chair and Teddy sat down. But after his couple minutes, he wouldn't move.

"I'm staying in the chair," he said.

"Teddy, if you don't get out of that chair, I'm going to push you over the side."

"You wouldn't dare," he said.

I had a firm foothold. I was standing on a big thick branch with my back against the trunk. We kept arguing and it came down to where he either was going to get out of the chair or I was going to push him over the side. I faked like I was going to push the chair with my foot, thinking that'd scare him. But it didn't. I had to do something now, so I kicked the chair easy. Real easy. I barely touched it. But we had nailed linoleum on the platform. With the wooden legs of the chair on it, the linoleum was really slick. That chair went zip, across the platform, with Teddy in it.

All of a sudden, Teddy and the chair weren't on the platform. They were in mid-air and he had the strangest expression on his face. He went "Ooooh" and his hat stayed there in mid-air for a split second when he dropped from under it.

Lucky for him, and lucky for me, there was a big brush pile on the ground underneath where the platform was. Teddy and the chair lit right in the middle of that brush pile. When they hit, that chair folded up with his ass and legs sticking out. But the brush pile saved him.

Another time, a couple years later, we conned Teddy into dressing up as a ghost with a big white sheet and a green wig.

At the time Harold Lees was the only kid in our group who drove a car. Whenever we went to the dances at the Catholic Youth Center, all the girls in our sophomore class went out afterwards with the older guys who had cars. So

one Friday night Teddy stayed home with his ghost cos-
tume while we spread the word among the girls that we
were going to a haunted house down the road near where
I lived. So a bunch of girls jumped in Harold's car with us.

It really was spooky along the dirt road. Halfway down
it, Harold pretended to stall the car, an old clutch-drive
'57 Ford.

From behind the house, Teddy came running out of
the bushes with his sheet flying and his green wig, yelling
"Aaaahhh, aaaahhh." In the car, the girls really started
screaming and jumping around. We were grabbing ass, we
thought that was a big deal then. And when Teddy reached
in the car to grab Jim Sailor, the girls were almost hysterical.

Two weeks in a row, Teddy did his act. But the next
Friday night, when Harold put the car in one of its stalls,
Teddy's mask slid crooked. Running blind, he ran smack
into a tail fin and flipped up onto the trunk. He almost
castrated himself. Harold didn't realize what had happened.
He put the car into first and stood on it. I yelled "Stop the
car, stop the car" but Harold banged it into second. By
now, Teddy was scratching on the rear window, trying to
hold on. But he slid back down into the road. His wig flew
off. His sheet ripped. He had gravel scrapes all over him.

Another time, Teddy's dad had a brand new '62 Buick
Special, a big heavy-duty job. It had that super low reduc-
tion gear where you could put it in low and squeal the tires
on the pavement.

We were at an age where we were really into cars.
Girls, cars, football, that's all we talked about. Most of us
knew how to drive but we weren't old enough to get a
license. Teddy's father knew Teddy could drive, but he had
saved for years to buy that car.

"Teddy," he told him, "don't you ever touch that car."

One day we were over at Teddy's house, watching him

mow the lawn. Everytime he stopped, somebody would suggest taking a ride in the new car, but Teddy kept shaking his head.

"I can't drive the car," he said. "My dad'll kill me."

Finally he got to where he had mowed all the grass except where the car was.

"You got to move it," I said. "You got to finish up."

"Yeah," he said. "I'll just move it a few feet over."

He went in the house to get the key. When he came out, his mother was right behind him.

"You better not drive that car," she was yelling. "You..."

She was still yelling when he started it up. He hit the accelerator but instead of moving forward, the car took off backwards. It hit a telephone pole so hard the taillights were bent around facing each other. His mother was really screaming now but Teddy didn't say a word. He just started running down the driveway. But he stopped, ran back into the house, and came out with a little bag. He ran past us down the driveway again and disappeared into the woods.

Teddy stayed away three days, until his father got so worried about him that he forgot about the car. Funny thing, but Teddy Augustyn is a long-distance trucker now. He drives for days and days, miles and miles.

One night my senior year in high school, I got home late after a Friday-night football game. I heard some voices in the fields out back near the railroad tracks. I thought it might be some hobos, so I thought I'd investigate. I went in the house, woke up my dad, and told him: "Somebody's out in the back fields. I'm going to see who it is."

I left the light on in my room. But when I got out in the fields, I discovered that the voices belonged to some buddies of mine who were sitting around a bonfire, drinking beer. I sat down with them, forgetting the light in my room was still on. Two hours later, when my dad woke up to go to work, he noticed the light and came out to investigate. He busted in on us with his shotgun.

"Why didn't you tell me you were here?" he said.

"I'm sorry, Dad," I said. "I just didn't think."

He walked back toward our farmhouse with a German shep, a dumb city dog. When a skunk ran out, the dumb dog thought it was a cat. He grabbed it and shook it by the scruff of the neck. The skunk pissed all over the dog and all over my dad. He had to take his clothes off in the backyard and wash himself in vinegar. But he couldn't get the skunk smell off his shoes. My dad raised hell about that then, especially when he had to wear those shoes to work. But he laughs about it now.

My dad and mom didn't have much money. But growing up, I had some great times that any kid would appreciate.

What bothers me is that my kids aren't getting the same things out of growing up that I did. They're supposed to be better off. I'm making good money. We've got a nice home on a nice block, with a swimming pool in the backyard. But my boys can't just roam the fields and woods like I did. They can't herd cows or go hunting and fishing like I did. And that's important for kids, especially boys. That's why I built an A-frame up in Franklin, North Carolina, near Asheville, just so I can give them a little of what my dad and mom gave me.

7

Tumbleweed and Bears

My mother always tells people that Wyoming was the only college that recognized my talent. But to tell you the truth, I didn't have very good grades in high school. My college boards weren't very good either. I stayed out late the night before I took them. I could hardly keep my eyes open. I wanted to go to Penn State but my grades and my college boards were far too low. Missouri was interested in me. Dan Devine, now the Green Bay Packers' coach, was the coach there then. He watched films of my games for Boonton, but he told people:

"The kid's a good player but the competition isn't very good in that league he's in."

I'd made All-County, but as a defensive back, not a running back. I thought my football career had ended with my last high school game. But out of nowhere, my coach, Joe Molitoris, got a phone call from one of the Wyoming assistant coaches. Wyoming was interested in another local running back, Dave Nigra of Passaic Valley. Watching films

*of him in a game against Boonton, the head coach had
noticed me. I didn't even know the head coach's name. It
was Lloyd Eaton, but at the time I'd never heard of him.*

*When the Wyoming letter-of-intent arrived in the
mail, I signed it. Like my mother says, Wyoming was the
only college that recognized my talent.*

I went to Syracuse, but my mom didn't care which
college I picked as long as I went to college. I didn't have
that many offers. I was All-County, but that was all. Stow
was a small school so I heard the same thing that Jim heard,
that the competition wasn't that good. But some other big
schools were interested in me. Clemson, Iowa, Vanderbilt.
At first my dad wanted me to go to Clemson because he
liked Frank Howard, the coach there. So did I, even when
he told me: "You damn Yankees, you don't eat grits and
you don't chew tobacco."

The only thing I didn't like about Clemson was that
there were only 300 girls to about 8,000 guys—then, anyway.
I wasn't that crazy about girls but I didn't like the idea of
not having hardly any around. I visited Iowa and one of
their assistant coaches took me up to Cleveland to see a
Browns game. That was 1963, the year Jimmy Brown got
the 1,863 yards, still the NFL record. It was the only time
I ever saw the Browns play when I was a kid. I only saw
the Indians play once.

*I used to go to baseball games at Yankee Stadium and
the Polo Grounds, then I'd hang around outside to get
autographs. The biggest autograph I ever got was Von Mc-
Daniel, a pitcher with the St. Louis Cardinals, and I almost
got Stan Musial but I missed him. That was my biggest
disappointment.*

I never was exposed to that as a kid. That's why I

enjoyed that trip to see the Browns so much. But then my parents got to know Ben Schwartzwalder, the Syracuse coach, and that was it. The night Ben visited the house, he and my father sat up drinking and telling war stories to each other. Ben had been a paratrooper. They were big buddies after that. Ben was no dummy.

Zonk was lucky. Syracuse wasn't that far from where he grew up. Wyoming was a big change for me.

The day I went out there for my freshman year, three of us went together—Dave Nigra, the running back from Passaic Valley, and George Galler from East Paterson, another running back. We flew to Denver, then we switched to Frontier Airlines to go to Cheyenne and then to Laramie, where the school is. After we took off from Cheyenne, we couldn't believe it. We were looking out the window at nothing. Absolutely nothing. Just desert and rocks. Then we saw this little town down below and we figured it must be the Laramie suburbs.

"We are now approaching Laramie," the pilot announced.

We couldn't believe it. We could see the whole town. That night we got settled in the dorm. The next day, a Saturday, we went into town. Tumbleweed was blowing across the main street. Believe me, it was tumbleweed. I'd seen enough Western movies in Jersey to know it was tumbleweed. And on a Saturday afternoon in Jersey, everybody would be out shopping. I expected it to be the same way in Laramie, but there was nobody downtown. Nobody. In a town of about twenty thousand people. Nobody.

They knew Jim had arrived.

If you were from the East, everybody out there thought you were a hood. Nicky Newark, they called me. The way I dressed, they really thought I had to be a gangster. All the guys out there wore T-shirts and jeans, white socks and cowboy boots. I walked around in Italian knit shirts with black silk pants and alpaca sweaters and sharp pointed shoes.

They didn't know if he was Robin Hood or Al Capone.

Everything I wore was monogrammed. JFK. My full name is James Forrest Kiick. I even had my underwear and my socks monogrammed.

If you'd come to Stow dressed like that, my boys in the Levis would've chopped you up.

As it turned out, I really enjoyed Wyoming my four years there. I met my wife Alice there. I met some very nice people. But at first I didn't like it at all. I couldn't stand the music on the radio. Country music on every station. It gave me headaches. And it really made me homesick. Dave Nigra couldn't take it. The second week, he left. I was on the freshman team but it was the same situation as in high school. I hardly played. Some of the other freshmen had been All-America high school players. I had been All-Morris County, defensive back. And here I wanted to be a running back.

One of the first days there, we got up a touch football game. They stuck me at center.

When the freshman games began, they used to throw the option pass and I played a little cornerback. I figured I was wasting my time. When I went home for Christmas, I almost didn't come back but I thought about what Kieffer Shriner had said about me being a quitter and I gave it another try. The second semester, things got better. Some of the other running backs left school, and another one was switched to defense. I had a good spring game and by then

I had made some good friends. I had a new roommate, Mike LaHood, and across the hall was Bob Aylward. The three of us really hung together. Like every Friday afternoon, we'd get some malt liquor, Colt 45, strong malt liquor. We'd take it up on Ninth Street hill and drink and talk until it was gone. We used to get pretty drunk. Then we'd go downtown and eat.

We called ourselves "The Me-Hoffs"—jack me-hoff, whip me-hoff, and beat me-hoff. "The Me-Hoffs."

It got so that everybody called us that, and we kept it alive. We considered ourselves to be like a singing group. We'd say, " 'The Me-Hoffs' are going to make a Christmas album." We couldn't sing but it gave us an identity. We even had a manager, Paul Toscano, our quarterback, who was drafted by the Houston Oilers as a defensive back. With that name and all, I was really living up to my hood image.

Jim knifed the first three guys he met out there. He rolled the president of the university.

I got along quite well with the coach there. Lloyd Eaton is a very good coach. He's with the Packers now as their player personnel director.

I don't regret going to Wyoming, but I never got into the cowboy thing out there.

On our away trips, we always wore big cowboy hats. They were really nice. You could keep them after your senior year. But when we came East to play Army, we landed at LaGuardia Airport in New York and I figured some of my boys from Lincoln Park might be there to meet me. I didn't dare wear my cowboy hat. I tucked it under my arm.

One of the things I liked best about Wyoming was the snow. My first varsity game, it snowed. It seemed like

it was always snowing. Sometimes all they used for trans-
portation was snowmobiles. Sometimes the snow was up
to the roof. Unbelievable.

I hated the snow at Syracuse, too. I hated the whole
area—Syracuse, Rochester, Buffalo, Cleveland, dismal gray
weather all the time. Anytime I hitchhiked between Syracuse and Cleveland on Interstate 90 in the winter, it
seemed like it was always snowing. Once, the only thing
moving on the entire stretch of Interstate 90 between
Syracuse and Cleveland was me and a New York state
trooper on a snowmobile, that's how bad it was.

I had been dropped off at an exit near Hamburg, New
York, and I was literally a walking snowman.

I was freezing. I was trudging along, hoping to see a
farmhouse where I could get warm. Just then, I heard a
snowmobile brrppping up behind me. The trooper slowed
down when he saw me. I hopped on behind him with my
suitcase and we took off to the next way station. Nothing
else was moving. Most of the trucks and cars were in the
way stations but some were stranded. In the way station,
people were sleeping on the floor and little kids were crying. I couldn't stand that. As cold as it was, I rode with
the trooper all night on the snowmobile, bringing coffee
and sandwiches to the truckers who were stranded.

The next day it cleared. I got a ride all the way to
Cleveland with one of the truckers, then I hitchhiked to
Stow.

I didn't like the weather at Syracuse but I liked the
football program. Ben Schwartzwalder was a tough old
bird, but I got along good with him. He was gruff. But so
were all the farmers I had worked for back in Stow, so Ben
was no problem for me. I knew that if I kept my mouth
shut and waited, he'd gruff himself out and then we could

talk. Like when he put me at middle linebacker in my sophomore season.

"I want to play fullback," I told him.

He didn't get irritated. He considered it, but he was more or less humoring me. So were the assistant coaches. They'd look at me and smile, like they were thinking, The kid wants to play fullback but there's no way. Even so, I kept reminding Ben that he recruited me as a fullback, that he had used me at fullback on the freshman team, that now I wanted a chance to play fullback on the varsity. The spot was open. Jim Nance had been a senior when I was a freshman, so he was with the Patriots when I got on the varsity. But there were a couple lettermen ahead of me. Ron Oyer was one, then he got hurt in the second game. Before the next practice, Ben called me aside.

"All right," he said, "I'm going to make a big move. I'm going to put you at fullback and let you stay there."

As always, I loved running the ball. Ben told me later, "Putting you at linebacker was one of the biggest mistakes I almost made." And when Ron Oyer came back, he was put behind Floyd Little at halfback. Ron Oyer is now the assistant athletic director at Syracuse, a good friend of mine. Half the reason they moved me over was to block for Floyd Little, but I didn't mind. I was getting my chance to run with the ball, too, even though I was a nobody. My sopho-more year, I had less than 800 yards. That wasn't much.

That's 200 yards more than my best year.

But at Syracuse we didn't throw the ball at all. Every play was up the middle or around the end. The publicity office pushed Floyd Little my sophomore and junior years, but I never resented it. Floyd was really nice to me. When he got invited to banquets, he always took me with him. Then, my senior year, the publicity office pushed me. I made

All-America. I also set the Syracuse career rushing record, which meant I gained more yards than Jimmy Brown or Ernie Davis or Jim Nance or Floyd Little had. In the game I set the record, I didn't even realize it. I was walking back to the huddle when the official handed me the ball.

"What's this for?" I asked him.

"For your trophy case," he said.

I still don't have a trophy case. That time, I just threw the ball toward the bench. It bounced around all crazy. They had to chase it. Now that I think about it, I should've at least carried it over there. I knew I was close to the record, but I never figured an official would stop the game and give me the ball. I've never been one for ceremonies. I just wanted to play football. Floyd Little was like that, too. He made me realize never to let the outside activities at college bother me. He wanted to play good football and get in the pros. That was his life. I made it my life, too. In my years in college, the hippie thing was beginning to move. The right wing. The left wing. There were a zillion things to be protesting.

Some of the guys on the team spread out into that, but Floyd never did. I never did, either.

One reason was that in January of my sophomore year, I married Pam. I hitchhiked home one weekend, borrowed a buddy's car, and Pam and I eloped. We drove up to Monroe, Michigan, on the west end of Lake Erie between Toledo and Detroit, and a preacher married us. I was raised a Catholic but I'm not much of a Catholic anymore. I'm a neutralist on religion now. At the time my dad thought I was a little young to get married. I was only nineteen and Pam was, too. But my mom thought it was great. She'd known Pam for a few years and she thought Pam was a great girl. She'd been afraid that when I went away to

Syracuse I wouldn't come home, that Pam and I would forget about each other. So she was really happy.

I don't believe Pam's folks were too thrilled. They wanted us to have a big June wedding, but rather than face the pressures involved in a large wedding, we eloped.

I brought Pam back to college with me, so I didn't care much about campus life after that. Like at the bonfire rallies my junior and senior years, I stood around wishing I was somewhere else. I didn't enjoy them. There wasn't anything there for me. I was married. I was busy trying to make some money.

I didn't read Dave Meggyesy's book, *Out of Their League*, but I'm told he wrote that some Syracuse players were collecting sixty dollars a month and that at least one had a free charge account at a men's store downtown. That was a few years before I got there, though. I don't know what those guys got or didn't get, but I know I never received anything like that, and I was in a real pinch for money. When Pam and I went home for Easter vacation, my junior year, we had twelve dollars in our savings account.

I knew Dave Meggyesy, too. Not well. But he grew up in Solon, Ohio, not too far from Stow, and his brother Dennis was at Syracuse when I was there. I'd see Dave at their house when his brother and I hitchhiked together. I never got into any philosophical discussions with him.

To earn the fifteen dollars a month that went with the tuition, room and board, books, and laundry on my athletic grant-in-aid, I mopped floors at night in the gym during the football season when I was a junior and a senior. I really mopped them, too.

After our wedding, I moved off campus, which meant I forfeited my room and board. I got a job as a night watchman in a parking lot, from eight at night to four in the morning. I did it during the football season, too. I was a walking zombie. Work all night. Go to classes. Go to practice. An alumnus helped me get the job but he didn't help me guard the parking lot. I got eighty dollars a week, and I earned it. I also needed it. I even did it one whole summer.

Nobody gave me a fancy car at Syracuse, either. The first car Pam and I owned was a '56 Chevrolet that was so many different colors, we called it our "Easter Egg" car. It had about eight owners before we got it. Wherever it had been scratched or banged up, it was painted a different color. The top was gray and brown and green. The body was mostly yellow with blue and gray and orange and green. And on the right front fender was a big purple spot.

It really burned oil. I always had to stop for oil before I stopped for gas. I kept a big can of crude oil in the trunk, I'd just pour it in like syrup.

It smoked but we loved that car. Going back to school one time, a state trooper stopped us. He didn't say a word. He just walked around our car looking at it. I knew he was thinking there was no way it could pass the safety test.

"Blink your lights," he said.

The lights worked. Then he walked around a little more, shaking his head. Finally he came over to my window.

"Go ahead, but take it easy."

My first car was a '56 Chevy, too. It had a fantastic radio but there was something wrong with the fuel pump. Going up a hill, the motor would sputter out. The only way I could go up a hill was in reverse.

But our "Easter Egg" car didn't last long. We took out a loan to buy a Pontiac Tempest that would be a little safer.

Up at Syracuse, the Adirondack Mountains weren't far away. I liked to go fishing and camping there. One time

Pam and I went camping with Ferg and Kitty, the couple next door in our apartment. Ferg was what people called a "hippie" then, with a beard and long hair. He thought he was an outdoorsman but he really wasn't. He was a city guy who'd read about the outdoors in magazines and books. For our trip, he had rented a big heavy canoe. We had to portage it half a mile to the lake from where we parked the car. Driving in on the logging road, we had seen a couple black bears.

"I guess," Ferg joked, "we'll have to arm-wrestle a bear for dinner."

After we lugged the canoe to the lake, I went back alone to the car to get the paddles. Returning to the lake I thought I'd crash through the bushes to save time. Not far from the lake, I stumbled into a clearing. Staring at me a few feet away was a she-bear with a cub. When the mother saw me, she stood up on her hind legs with her fangs out. She had her claws out, too, with her palms up, ready to swat me. Her claws were out about two inches. They looked like half-penny nails.

I dropped the paddles. I wanted her to think I was leaving. But as I backed into the bushes, I stepped on another cub. When it squealed, the mother came at me.

By now I was running as fast as I could through the brush toward the lake, yelling, "Ferg, Ferg." I knew he had brought a .38 with him. I was hoping he'd see the bear and fire a shot to scare her away. But he thought I was screwing around. He didn't know I had to run into the lake to save my ass. The bear stopped at the edge of the lake, growled for a couple minutes, and then wandered back into the woods to her cubs. Pam, Ferg, and Kitty had been safe enough and so was I, now, but I didn't go back to get those paddles until the next morning.

I had another experience with a bear up in Canada, where I like to go camping every year before reporting to training camp.

We had our tent pitched on the edge of a lake. One morning just as dawn was breaking, I woke up with this weight bumping against me from outside the tent. I thought it was my brother Joe or my father-in-law, Chuck Conley, fooling around again. I pushed whoever it was with my elbow. But then I happened to glance over inside the tent. My brother and father-in-law were still sleeping. I peeked outside, and a bear was wobbling into the bushes.

Get the hat. Zonk elbowed a bear. Get the hat.

When we got up and looked around, we figured the bear had been licking the bottom of a greasy frying pan.

Zonk elbowed a bear.

Any bears in Wyoming?

I never got into the camping thing. I was too busy playing pool. Our dorm was at one end of the campus, away from most of the classrooms. In between was the Student Union, where the pool tables were. It was always quite cold in Wyoming, so on the way to class I always stopped in the poolroom to get warm. There'd always be a game going on. It seemed like I always got involved. By the time I finished, it was time for football practice. I'd blown the whole day.

New Jersey Fats.

In high school, when we had assembly on Friday mornings, we sneaked down to Piontek's poolroom. Tony Strelec was a rack boy there. He had a key. It was a real poolroom. Smoky, dingy. Not like the fancy ones now. It was my second home. One time I had about twenty dollars on me to buy Christmas presents. I almost lost it all but I came out ahead. I ended up buying more presents for everybody. Other times I didn't come out so well. I'd have to hitch-hike the five miles home. But usually I won.

The hustler.

Vic Washington, who's now with the San Francisco 49ers, was a year behind me at Wyoming and he was from New Jersey, too. Plainfield, not too far from me. We played pool all the time. Most of the guys who played were from back East, and we usually won. The guys from Wyoming usually lost. I financed my dates with Alice with the money I won.

Alice Chaussart was a cheerleader in high school in Laramie, a junior when I met her. I was a freshman.

I chased her, which I don't like to admit. I was always calling her up, looking for her, waiting for her to come out of a class, which is something that girls usually do. But she wanted no part of me. Her father had died of a heart attack when she was about six and her mother died of cancer the year I met her. Her mother's friends and her three sisters were telling her, "Don't go out with him." They really thought I was a hood.

They were right.

They were telling her, "We'll get him plane fare, we'll fly him back to New Jersey," and I told them, "Fine, you get the plane fare and I will fly home." They were just kidding, I think, but if they'd got the money up, I would've been gone. But me and Alice didn't get too involved then. After my sophomore year, I just figured I was going home to have a good summer and forget about her.

I really had a fantastic time. I lifted weights, drank beer, ate pizza, went to fights.

Not boxing matches. Brawls. We had fights all the time at the dances we went to. We drank beer in big containers we called bumpers. We played donkeyball, something like handball, all hours of the night behind the school with a little fifteen-cent red ball. That's what I'd always wanted to do. And all that summer I did it.

My junior year, I stopped chasing her. Alice wondered what was going on. But then we got together again. We really began to get serious when I began talking about becoming a Catholic convert. Her family is Catholic, very religious. I had gone to Sunday School in the Reformed Church in America as a boy, but I wasn't religious at all.

The thing that got me interested in converting was a religion course I was taking at Wyoming then. It seemed like other people just went to church, but Catholics believed more and did more. I have my doubts now the other way. I think Catholics get carried away too much. I think everybody gets carried away too much by religion.

But partly because of my thinking then, and partly because Alice is a Catholic, I became a convert.

I haven't stuck with it. I don't really consider myself to be a Catholic now. I believe, I think, in God but not all the other stuff that Catholics are supposed to believe in. It's nothing I regret having done, though.

When we got engaged, my mother got all shook up. She hadn't met Alice, but that didn't bother her as much as she didn't think I was ready to get married.

Back home, I was never really involved with girls. I didn't go to the prom. I hadn't gone steady with anybody. My mother thought it was a case of my first love. It was a big shock to her. She was upset. I told her: "I want you to come out for the wedding. But if you don't come out, I'm still going to get married."

My mother and father came out for the wedding in

June of my junior year. My mother and Alice get along great. She likes Alice better than she likes me. It's funny, because my mother's name is Alice, too.

Jim argues with one Alice in Miami, then he goes to Lincoln Park and argues with both of them.

I'm still carefree. Very carefree. That's the way I am. I don't worry about many things. That bugs Alice and it bugs my mother. But it's just the way I am. I really enjoy having a good time. Just relaxing. One of the few times in my life I didn't relax was the day of the NFL draft, maybe the longest day of my life. I was with Bob Aylward in the Student Union that morning. He had to go over to Cheyenne to get a Volkswagen bus. I went with him, because I didn't want to sit around waiting to see which team drafted me in which round. When we got back, I asked Alice: "Any phone calls?"

Just from the look on her face, I knew there hadn't been any. I was just so disappointed. The year before, when I had a big game in the Sun Bowl, some scouts told me that if I'd been eligible then, I'd have been drafted in the first round. But now, on the day of my draft, I knew they had gone through at least four rounds. At about eight-thirty that night, I was watching TV when the phone rang.

"Jim, this is Joe Thomas of the Miami Dolphins," the voice said. "We've drafted you on the fifth round. We think you'll help us. We'll be in contact with you."

It was that quick. I didn't know whether to be happy or not. I'd always wanted to play for one of the New York teams, but I hadn't counted on it because there were twenty-six teams that could draft me. When the Dolphins took me, I realized I didn't know that much about them. It was a day I'd never want to go through again. It was just terrible. All you can do is sit and wait.

I was lucky. I didn't have to wait that long. I just wanted to be drafted by a team in a city where it was warm. I thought the Rams might take me. Their people had talked to me at the East-West Shrine game and the Hula Bowl. Joe Thomas had talked to me. So had somebody from the Cowboys and the Buffalo Bills, but I'd had enough of that Buffalo weather my four years at Syracuse.

"I really don't want to play in Buffalo," I said.

I hated that area. I was so sick of it always being wet, cold, sloppy, freezing, snowing. We had so much snow at Syracuse one time, I couldn't get my car up the driveway. I outgrew snow when I got a car. The day of the draft, Alan Brickman, the attorney who had offered to handle my contract, had me in his office when the phone rang. He listened for a few seconds, then turned to me.

"Miami," he said. "You were the first running back taken, the eighth player in the first round."

I smiled. I'd hardly heard of the Dolphins but at least the weather would be warm. The thing was, the Dolphins and the Bills had been tied for the eighth and ninth picks in that draft. The Dolphins won a coin-toss to go eighth. Then the Bills took Haven Moses, a wide receiver from San Diego State.

My four years at Syracuse, that coin-toss and Ben Schwartzwalder's decision to put me at fullback were more important to me than any course.

As a football player, I got an easy ride on marks on easy courses. I was a physical education major. But I took some tough courses, too, like business administration. I took four years of English, too. I liked English literature. I did very well in courses I liked. The ones I didn't like, I didn't make time for. I'm still a semester and a half short of my degree. I don't have any regrets now, but I've been lucky. Like if I'd gotten hurt and never made it into the pros, I'd need that degree.

Pro football is nice. I enjoy the notoriety, but a pro football player is living in limbo. Eventually he's going to have to go out into the real world and get a real job. I'm looking to get into real estate and land development. I've taken courses at the University of Fort Lauderdale with that in mind.

I learned a lot about people at college, about how money really was important to some people. On the farm, I never thought that much about having money or not having it. But at Syracuse, I was around individuals whose fathers really had a lot of money. These people had money, new cars, new clothes. Their having it didn't bother me, but when they made a point of letting me know they had it, that bothered me a great deal. I really resented that. On the farm, an old car had meant as much to me as a new car.

We didn't have many rich kids at Wyoming, but the big thing I got out of going there was realizing that people were different. They acted different, they dressed different, they lived different, they cared about different things. Me and my friends in Lincoln Park, we just cared about sports. I learned about people at Wyoming, but I didn't graduate either. I'm a year short. I wanted to take medical technology but I was told I couldn't handle it, I guess because of my high school grades.

I was put in phys ed. I was a point from being on the dean's list my freshman year. All of a sudden it didn't appeal to me at all. I didn't want to be a phys ed teacher. History courses interested me. So did zoology. But to hear about education bored me. I have a good memory, so I always got by. The night before an exam, I'd study and remember enough to get by.

Looking to when I'm through playing football, if I had a wish I'd be a singer. I love music. Except that as far as talent goes, I couldn't handle it. I'd like to have a bar.

I'd like to be able to walk in and say, "Buy that guy a drink." The clothing business interests me, too. But whatever I do, I want to be my own boss. I've been lucky, because if I hadn't played football, I'd probably be in Lincoln Park now, just hanging around.

And if I hadn't gone to Syracuse, I might be a line-backer somewhere now. Or back on the farm.

My last year at Syracuse, the coaches were trying to recruit Walt Patulski, who later was an All-America defensive end at Notre Dame and the number one choice in the 1972 draft by the Buffalo Bills. But at Christian Brothers Academy in Syracuse, he had been a great running back. He's 6-5 and 265 now. He wasn't that big then, maybe 6-3 and 235. The coaches asked me to talk to him.

"I want to be a running back," he told me.

"Then come here," I said. "I proved that a guy our size can be a running back. The coaches will give you a chance here."

"They promised me a chance at Notre Dame."

But as a freshman there, he was switched to defensive end. The whole point is, Walt Patulski will never know if he could've made it as a running back.

8

The Rookies

Our first meal at the College All-Star camp, I was sitting at a table in the old Evanston Hotel when a huge guy walked by. I figured he had to be a lineman.

"That's Csonka," somebody said.

I couldn't believe the size of him. With the exception of a couple linemen at Wyoming, I had been bigger than anybody else on the team. Zonk was the biggest person I'd ever seen who was a running back. I started to wonder what the hell I was doing there. I'm still wondering because the All-Star coach that year, Norm Van Brocklin, didn't use me in the game. Not even for one play. Not even on any of the kickoffs or punts.

Jim had a bad attitude.

But we had a good time. The first night, me and Zonk went out with a few other guys and we got talking. That's the first time we were together. We were out drinking.

We were out drinking every night.

There was a curfew but nobody paid any attention to it. Everybody sneaked down the hotel fire escape, the kind with the ladder that swings down to the sidewalk and then swings back up. If it wasn't for the College All-Stars, that old fire escape probably would rust away. But the town of Evanston itself isn't much. I walked half an hour looking for a bar until I found out it was a dry town. None of the guys took the game seriously. At least none I knew.

Something was happening every night.

Like with Mo Moorman and the mustard.

We had been out drinking with Mo, the big guard who's now with the Chiefs, and about four in the morning we stopped in a Toddle House for hamburgers. The lady behind the counter was so busy, she was really bitching. Then she bitched at Mo about something.

Mo took the mustard, one of those plastic squeeze jobs, and aimed it at her.

"You do that," she hissed, "I'll call the cops. You do that, you're in jail."

Mo didn't even change expression. He just squeezed it slow. He shot her across the dress, and he kept going across the ovens, the grill, and everything else behind the counter. She yelled "You big bastard," and then she went for the phone to call the police. I'd just been served my hamburgers. As we ran out, I was eating one hamburger and holding the other one.

We didn't go back there.

Mo was really something.

One night we went down to Old Town in Chicago and

he was driving. Somehow we got in an alley that was a dead end, but Mo just took a left on the sidewalk. Another night when we were drinking, he picked up one of those black plastic ashtrays you always see in bars. With one hand, he squeezed it. And it broke. It just cracked in two. I figured, Hell, it can't be so tough. When he wasn't looking, I squeezed it with one hand. Nothing. With two hands. Nothing. I sneaked it back on the table and forgot about it.

Somebody always had a party to go to.

One party, when we walked up to the front door, some guy we didn't know was standing at the window with no clothes on. We walked in and Wayne Meylan was sitting in a chair with a quart of bourbon.

Wayne Meylan was a nice guy but he looked like evil walking.

He was a linebacker from Nebraska, a farmer, a jutted jaw.

He was a nice guy but he was tough. He was toughness embodied. He'd tackle you and just about kill you. When he got drunk, he just got numb. At this party, he was pretty numb when we walked in. He didn't know it, but he was on his way to drinking that whole bottle of bourbon by himself. Straight. No ice. No nothing.

The bottle was being passed around, but the others were only pretending to take a drink. When the bottle got back to Wayne, he would take another drink. Finally he was sitting there, looking straight ahead but his eyes weren't focusing, when he said: "I'm going to die. Take me to the hospital."

Me and George Daney, a big lineman from Texas–El Paso who went to the Chiefs, took him to the hospital. We stayed there an hour with him, then we took him back to the hotel. The next day, I never saw a guy look so bad. He wasn't right for about three days.

Jim Cox kept things happening. He was a tight end the Dolphins had drafted out of the University of Miami.

I met him at picture day. We had to get dressed up in our uniforms with the stars on it for the photographers and the TV crews in the Chicago area. Nobody bothered taking pictures of me and Cox, so we were sitting over by ourselves on the bench when he started talking out loud: "I'm Jim Cox, All-America, Miami, you want me?"

He went through all the records he'd set, all the honors he'd received. He really had me laughing. After a while, one of the photographers looked over. I guess he thought we were a little crazy.

"I'm Jim Cox, All-America, Miami," he repeated.

The photographer looked away quick, packed up his stuff, and got out of there as fast as he could.

"I'm Jim Cox, All-America, Miami, you want me?"

I remember Cox doing that. He had all those photographers shook up. I thought he was a helluva dude then, but until then I hadn't been too sure. I knew his roommate, Bob Tatarek, from the Coaches All-America game in Atlanta and Bob had gone to the University of Miami, too. They put him and Cox together. Bob asked me to stop by his room with him, but just as we got near it I heard a muffled gun blast. Then four more.

"What the hell is all that?" I asked him.

"That's just Cox with his .38."

Cox had seen so many Elliott Ness shows on TV, he figured he'd need a .38 in Chicago for protection. To see what it would do, he had taken two telephone books, put them on the bed, put a pillow around them, and shot five holes in them.

One night me and Cox got back late, but when we got to the fire escape the ladder wouldn't come down. We had to walk in the front door.

The reason the ladder wouldn't come down was that I fell off it going out that night. I crashed into some garbage cans. Scared hell out of an old man in the alley. And when I fell off the ladder, the spring must've broken. The ladder swung back up, but it wouldn't swing down anymore. It didn't make that much difference. The guys just came and went as they pleased. We were supposed to have a curfew but nobody checked. And the coach, Norm Van Brocklin, didn't seem to care.

Don't mention his name.

Jim's favorite coach.

One day he was in a good mood, the next day he wasn't. One meeting, he told us to go out and have a good time that night. Another time he blew up when Oscar Reed, the running back with the Vikings now, walked in a minute late. Nobody knew what he was going to do next.

Van Brocklin pouted all the time. He acted like nobody ever wanted to do it his way.

My mistake was thinking I'd get in shape at the All-Star camp, so I didn't report in good shape. I had been home all summer, drinking beer and eating pizza. And hell, I wasn't All-America or anything like that, just All-Western Athletic Conference, and I'd played in the Senior Bowl game. So when I reported, I wasn't very impressive. My time for the 40 wasn't too good. Van Brocklin wanted to move me to fullback.

"Not me," I said. "I won't be playing fullback with the Dolphins."

"You should want to play anywhere," he said. "You've got a bad attitude."

Now why would a coach ever think that you had a bad attitude?

He fixed me. He didn't use me in the game. The hardest hit I took was when Curley Culp, the defensive tackle now with the Chiefs, bumped into me when he ran out of bounds trying to tackle one of the Green Bay Packers at the sideline.

I didn't take that game too seriously.

You must've taken it a little seriously. You won that big trophy as the All-Stars' most valuable player.

The Packers beat us, 34–17; I remember that.

The only thing I remember was a beautiful girl sitting in the fourth row behind our bench. Dark black hair. Really nice. I was so pissed off about not playing, I hardly watched the game. I just watched her.

I was surprised that the Packers didn't hit me any harder than I'd been hit in college. One time Ray Nitschke just smiled at me, a friendly smile, not a mean smile. That's when I realized the pros were people.

Vince Lombardi thought Zonk was too slow.

That's the way it came out in the papers, but I was told later that he never really said that. I never talked to him about it. The only time I met him was in 1970 when he made a shaving-cream commercial with Charley Taylor when he was the Redskins' coach. The commercial was filmed in the Orange Bowl and me and Jim were a couple extras in it.

We each got fifty dollars for eight hours as extras that day.

That was the last time we saw him before he died.

Besides that girl in the fourth row at the All-Star game, I remember they let us keep our jerseys. I didn't even have to clean mine. The next day, when me and Zonk and Jim Cox went to join the Dolphins, it was folded in my bag like a clean shirt. In those years, when George Wilson was the coach, the Dolphins trained in Boca Raton, about thirty miles north of Miami, at St. Andrew's school. When we got there, we discovered we were roommates. Walking to the dorm, the first player we ran into was Ray Jacobs, a big defensive tackle who had been around. When he saw me and Zonk, he looked us up and down.

"Fuckin' rookies," he said. "Fuckin' prima donna rookies."

I thought, Oh shit. At the time we didn't know his name. But just looking at him, we knew he was a veteran. And just to let us know that he meant what he said, he spit on Zonk's shoes.

He meant to spit near them, but he hit them.

Zonk didn't even challenge him about that.

At that point, all I wanted to do was go to the room. Ray Jacobs was a moose, he was huge. He was about 285, about 6-3, and tough. We found out later that when he was home in Texas he hunted rattlesnakes. At training camp, he hunted rookies.

Giblet-ass, they called him. He had no ass.

He was all upper body and stomach. He came across as a tough guy, a really harsh talker. But once we got to know him, he wasn't that way at all. He was a friendly, happy-go-lucky guy, a helluva guy, a real thoughtful guy. After my rookie year, we went around selling season tickets together. He had a hard time remembering people's names, so he just called everybody "Cuz." He'd say, "Hi, Cuz." We just didn't know him that first day.

When we got to our room, there was a little white card on the door. "Csonka and Kiick." I'll never forget that.

That night, they had the rookie show. The rookies put on a few skits but Jim and I weren't in them because we'd just arrived. We hadn't had time to rehearse. But they had me opening and shutting the curtain. I was their number one draft choice. They made sure I wasn't sitting around.

Joe Mirto, a guard from the University of Miami, was on the stage, smoking a cigar in a portable john. "Jokes from the John," they called it. Every once in a while, he'd pop open the door and say something funny about the coaches. But he'd never smoked before. He got so sick.

Then we had the rookie party.

And we all got sick at that.

When we were rookies, the Dolphins had a lot of veterans who had been around the old American Football League for years. Guys like Wahoo McDaniel, John Bramlett, Mel Branch, Ray Jacobs, Tom Nomina, they really knew how to have a rookie party. They took us out drinking two nights in a row at a bar down near the ocean. They tried to kill us. The first night, they took me out behind the bar onto this little bridge about thirty feet over the beach.

"All right, Zonk," somebody ordered. "Dive."

I was so drunk I didn't even look. I did a one-and-a-half gainer off that bridge. But there was no water down there. I landed head first on the beach and knocked myself cold. The second night was worse. They had me and Randall Edmunds chugalugging tequila. Randall Edmunds was a rookie linebacker from Georgia Tech who had never had a drink in his life. Until that night. At the bar, Stan Mitchell, one of the veteran running backs, stood behind me, like he was in my corner at a fight.

"Now listen, Zonk," he .was saying. "You've got to beat this guy. The offense has got to beat the defense."

I nodded, "Yeah, okay, Stan, sure." I'd had a few drinks. I wasn't too sure where I was coming from, but I knew Randall Edmunds had never had a drink. I knew I'd handle him, that he'd upchuck right away. Hell, growing up on the farm, I'd been drinking for years.

On the bar, a little jigger glass was in front of each of us. The barmaid was pouring tequila into them.

I took mine and tossed it down. Randall took his, smelled it, swallowed it, looked at me and smiled. I thought, Hell, two'll get him. But he kept drinking them down and looking straight ahead and smiling at me. On the ninth shot, I upchucked. I really upchucked. I hit the barmaid, I turned and hit Stan, I hit some stranger who was just watching, I opened the door and hit a couple walking in; outside I hit a convertible parked there. The last thing I remember, I was laying in the parking lot, thinking about Randall Edmunds never having a drink before. But he was still standing in the bar, smiling at me.

Stan Mitchell took me back to camp, undressed me, sat me under the shower, and turned on the cold water. That's when I woke up. Two minutes later, Jim came crawling in and sat under the next shower.

I was the number one draft choice's roommate so I got a hard time, too. I had been drinking beer with shots of white lightning, real moonshine. Chugalug. The loser had to do it again. You should've seen us the next day at our first practice. We figured George Wilson knew there had been a party, that he wouldn't make us run. When he blew his whistle, we gathered around him and he said: "All the veterans . . ."

We thought, What a nice guy, he's going to make the veterans run, not the rookies. Then he finished the sentence: ". . . go over and sit down."

We knew what he was going to say now, and he said it. "Rookies, start running."

Me and Zonk were dying. Just dying. The only reason we made it was because we were still half drunk.

We had to run a mile and a half. Guys were stopping along the way, upchucking. But somehow we made it.

Then we had to run the ropes. Every couple feet, there were ropes stretched across, about a foot off the ground. The idea is to make you step high. I don't know about Zonk, but when I was standing in line, waiting to go, it looked like the ropes were moving.

Swaying. The whole practice field was swaying.

When it was our turn, I started running but I tripped. So did Zonk behind me. We kept tripping and falling in the ropes. It was terrible. I heard people saying, "Who are those two rookies?" It was just terrible.

But as terrible as we were, something good came out of it. George Wilson told me: "You're all right, kid. The front office told me you were a prick, but you're all right."

Joe Thomas, then the Dolphins' personnel director and now the Baltimore Colts' general manager, hadn't liked the way I had stuck with my attorney, Alan Brickman of Syracuse, in my contract negotiations. I let Alan call the shots and Joe resented that. But the thing that impressed me about George Wilson was that he saw through whatever Thomas had told him.

After the rookie party and that first morning practice, the veterans didn't harass us much.

Or if they did, we spoke up. They liked that. I think they were hoping to get us to speak up.

Like the time Tom Goode got on me. He was a big tobacco-chewer from Mississippi, a center. One day he noticed me in my shiny black pants. He shook his head and said: "If you dressed like that where I come from, they'd run you out of town."
He had on jeans with white socks and a white T-shirt, so I said to him: "If you dressed like that where I come from, they'd run you out of town."

He always liked Jim after that. He was a tough guy. He had torn cartilage in his knee, torn cartilage in his ankle. He had bone chips in his wrist from a fracture he thought had just been a sprain. He had a shoulder that was banged up. He must've had eight injuries that other guys would've pulled up with, but he not only kept playing with them, he never complained about them. I really got to like Tom Goode because he woke up early like I do. When we had an exhibition game in Miami, we'd be the first two up at training camp, long before it was time for breakfast. I'd meet him in the Howard Johnson's and we'd each drink a pot of coffee and talk. When he got traded to the Colts in 1970, he finally had a big moment of glory. Tom was the center who snapped the ball for Jim O'Brien's field goal that won the Super Bowl that season.

Me and Zonk used to room next to Tom and Mel Branch, a big defensive end. They had a real brass spittoon in their room. They'd sit there, chewing tobacco and playing the guitar and singing the old songs.

We had a little defensive back, Bob Neff, who could really sing. When Tom and Mel would come in drunk, they'd go wake up Neff and bring him down to their room. Neff would sing while Tom and Mel clapped and howled like old hound dogs.

We got along with the veterans real good. Zonk got along with Joe Auer so good, he almost got killed.

Joe Auer was a running back who was the Dolphins' first star. In their very first game in 1966, he ran the opening kickoff back 95 yards for a touchdown. But he was famous for other things, too. Like before we knew him, he had a pet lion. Its name was Clifford and it lived in Joe's house with him. It ripped up the house a few times.

"Clifford didn't really know he was a lion," Joe told me once. "I got him when he was a kitten, maybe fifteen pounds. I had to teach him to growl. I'd get down on my knees and go 'Grrr, grrr,' and he finally caught on. It takes them about four years to realize they're lions. I finally had to get rid of him, but he wasn't dangerous."

Joe was more dangerous. Especially when he was driving his dune buggy.

Joe was one of the old fraternal football players, a helluvan athlete, fast and strong. But he didn't like to practice. He liked good times. That's the way he lived. He had this dune buggy that was a chopped-down Volkswagen with a roll bar and a plasticized body. He liked to drive that dune buggy flat out. To him it was a Maserati, not a dune buggy. One night he was driving it flat out into a right-angle turn on the road leading into training camp. He had been spinning and sliding it on the sand on the side of the road, and I knew he was going too fast to make the turn. I yelled: "Joe, you're going to roll this thing over on us."

"No way, Zonk," he said. "No way it'll roll over."

Sure as hell, when he hit that turn, it rolled over. The windshield came out. I came out. Joe came out. The dune buggy did a complete somersault, landed on its wheels, and kept going up through the palmettos. Whooor, whooor, it was disappearing into the bushes when I yelled: "Joe, it's going to sink in the swamp there."

He loved that dune buggy. But now that it had rolled over on him, he stood up, blood all over the side of his face. Watching it plow through the palmettos, he said: "Fuck the dune buggy."

We walked the rest of the way.

But the next cut, Joe was gone.

I had thought the veteran running backs wouldn't be very friendly to me and Jim, but it wasn't that way at all. Joe Auer was great while he lasted. So was Jack Harper, who came up with a pinched nerve in his neck.

That's how I got my chance to play.

Stan Mitchell was a great guy. Easy-going. Big ol' brown eyes, a lady killer from Tennessee in a soft hillbilly way. He had women fighting over him, literally fighting over him. He really needed a woman to take care of him. There must've been twenty fighting to do it. Instead of washing his clothes, Stan just stuffed them into the back seat of his car, right up to the window. When it came time to go on a road trip, he'd go around to all the rookies' rooms and borrow whatever clothes he needed without telling anybody. He must've taken ten of my ties, probably that many shirts too.

One time when my brother Joe was visiting me, we were riding with Stan in his car with a big stack of dirty laundry in the back seat. On the radio he had Hank Williams, the famous country singer. Stan really loved him. He really loved country music. My brother turned to Stan and said: "How did Hank Williams die?"

Stan turned to him with a sorry look on his face and said quietly: "People say he died of a broken heart."

"Mitchell," I said, "stop this car and let me out. I don't mind your stinky dirty laundry and I don't mind that goddamn music. But when you give me that horseshit, I want out."

Hank Williams had a bad heart. But when he died at twenty-nine, liquor and pills were mentioned, too. But that was Stan.

Billy Neighbors was another veteran we got along good with. Billy was a guard who had been with the Boston Patriots when they were a good team. He was a great guy but he was one of the biggest bullshitters I've ever known. On plane trips, he'd look down at the farmland or mountains, and say: "Look at those eels down there. They're crawling out to California and back. It's a phenomenon not many people know."

Not many people knew what Billy was talking about half the time, either. No matter what the subject was, like if it was how air pollution was causing cancer in ants, Billy knew all about it. My rookie year, me, Dick Anderson and Bob Petrella drove to work with him every day when we practiced at Miami Stadium, the baseball park. When something came up in the conversation, Dick Anderson usually knew what he was talking about. Billy didn't but he pretended to.

"Oh, yes," Billy would say. "I read about that in the Wall Street Journal last week. According to their research . . ."

He'd keep talking, reciting statistics, everything. But he had made up everything. Dick Anderson would get so mad, because he really knew something about it but Billy had bullshitted him.

Billy never let his stomach out. He had a little paunch, and whenever he walked around he always had it pulled way in.

Billy was known for his calisthenics—that is, he was known for not doing them with everybody else when practice started.

One time somebody conned Billy into doing sit-ups. He did two, then he jumped up and gasped, "All right, that's enough."

When we played in Denver our rookie year, we went out to buy some cowboy boots but Billy sat in the store, holding the boots and huffing and puffing.

"I can't get one on," he said. "My foot's too big."

His problem was that he didn't have any shank above his ankle. His calf muscle sat right on top of his ankle. His ankles were really thick.

"Your foot's not too big," I said. "Your leg's too short."

Billy's chest is so big he can't play golf. He can't come around with a club like you're supposed to. But the biggest guy on the team that year was another guard, Charlie Fowler, the Miami Dolphins' all-time eating champion.

Charley Fowler lived for food.

Charley ate everything he saw.

One time in Boston we went to Anthony's Pier IV restaurant down by the harbor. He ordered the clambake special—steamed clams, lobster, corn, the whole thing. While we were waiting, Charley went through the celery, carrots and olives, and the bread. The waitress brought us big fluffy popover rolls. He ate his and a few others. Then he went through another basket of bread. When the steamed clams and the lobster and the corn came, he polished them off. Then he ate most of somebody else's lobster and half of my steak. He topped it off with about three desserts.

Charley Fowler could go from 260 to 280 in a meal.

After that, I didn't go out to eat with Charley if I could avoid it. He was a nice guy but watching him eat made me feel bad. He wasn't a sloppy eater, he was just consistent. He ate everything.

When we practiced at Miami Stadium our rookie year, we went to the S and S cafeteria for lunch. Charley ate the whole counter.

We got along with the veterans better than we did with some of the rookies. But that was because some rookies were different than we were, like John Boynton—a big lean tackle from Tennessee, one of the strongest, quietest guys I've ever known. I don't believe I ever heard him open his mouth, not even to say "Hi." But he wasn't mean, he was just quiet. Stan Mitchell, who was from Tennessee too, told me: "John's from the real backwoods. Where he lives, you just don't walk down in where his house is without knowing somebody there."

John didn't scowl. He just was quiet. But just looking at him, you knew you didn't want to mess with him. One guy tried, Norm McBride, a big defensive end. They got into a fight and Boynton hit him so hard, McBride actually screamed because he thought his jaw was broken. Boynton just stared at him.

Bob Joswick was the weirdest rookie in our group.

He'd drive you crazy, a defensive end from Tulsa.

He spent all his time thinking of stupid jokes. At practice, he'd put his face against your shoulder and say, "I've got my eye on you." Or he'd whack you on the back and say, "Glad you're back."

But once the season started, it seemed like we weren't rookies anymore.

Not that many rookies make a team to stay. There are only five of us on the Dolphins now who were rookies that year—me and Zonk and Doug Crusan on offense, Manny Fernandez and Dick Anderson on defense. But that's a pretty good five.

Doug Crusan is one of the NFL's best offensive tackles. On the field, he's all business. But off it, he's the team clown.

Like when we're watching films, everybody falls asleep at one time or another. But before the lights go out, Doug will take a big spray can and spray the meeting room.
"The Anti-Z Monster Spray," he calls it.

The Z-Monster, of course, is what puts you to sleep. Watching films, even Shula gets sleepy sometimes. He doesn't actually fall asleep. But when he gets sleepy, he stands up and shuffles around to stay awake. You know he's as sleepy as everybody else, but he's the coach so he can get up and make it look like he's thinking.

During the films once, Shula caught me. "Wake up, wake up," he said and nudged me. But the coaches make us watch films at a bad time. Right after lunch. I always feel like taking a nap then. When the lights go off, the Z-Monster always gets me. When the lights go on and we're walking out, Doug Crusan will look around.

"Who did the Z-Monster get today?" he'll say.

Doug loves to make people laugh. One time at training camp when George Wilson was the coach, a girl society reporter visited us to write about the "animals" who play football. She was sitting at George's table at lunch when she burst out laughing.

For dessert that day, we had jello with whipped cream. Crusan had scooped up the whipped cream from about six jellos and plopped it all over his face.

Doug really had that girl reporter laughing. That's why he did it. His lifelong ambition is to be one of the clowns on a kiddie show on television.

His idols are the Banana Splits, the TV cartoon comedians. He'll sit in his room at training camp, watching the Banana Splits and laughing. You've got to picture this guy, 6-6, 260, a huge body but a tiny head. That's why the guys call him Bluto, after the character in the Popeye cartoon.

Doug made that girl reporter realize that football players aren't "animals" at all. He ruined her story.

All that talk about football players being "animals" is strictly bullshit. Some players might use it as a joke, to fool people on the outer edges of football or the general public.

But they never fool another jock. Football players are like everybody else. They're flesh and bone. You can't come on like a dragon all the time.

Some people who aren't football players act more like "animals" to me. Like politicians.

Most players are as professional in their job as doctors or lawyers, like Manny Fernandez, our big defensive tackle who did such a great job stopping Larry Brown when we won the Super Bowl game. The year we were rookies, Manny hadn't even been drafted. He was signed as a free agent out of Utah because the Dolphins thought that with his name he'd sell tickets to the Cuban population.

"I'm sorry," he said after he'd signed. "I can't speak Spanish."

He had been a good college player but nothing special. I think he was just cut out to be a pro. He doesn't go for the rah-rah that some college coaches demand. Just put him in the defensive line, tell him to kill the quarterback or stop a running back, and he'll do it. He knows what he's doing out there. He's a very bright guy, the professional type. He's in complete control of himself. He's a complete professional.

All us rookies blended in with the veterans pretty quickly that year. But of all the veterans, John Bramlett was my man. John Bramlett is almost a whole chapter by himself.

9

The Bull, Wahoo, and Riley

My rookie year, John Bramlett took me under his wing.

There are a helluva lot safer spots to be than under John Bramlett's wing.

He did drink a little bit too much. He went to extremes.

Bourbon. Scotch. Beer. He drank everything and anything.

But he was the best drinker I've ever seen as far as not passing out is concerned. I never saw him get sick. But when he drank he got a little wild. He was a linebacker from Memphis State who had played with the Denver Broncos until he was traded to the Dolphins the year before me and Zonk arrived. He and his wife lived upstairs from me and Alice in the Villa apartments. We were up there for dinner so often, he wanted to write us off on his income tax as dependents. When he wasn't drinking, he'd do anything for you.

Except that he was drinking most of the time.

He was wild to begin with. As a kid growing up in Memphis, he was in the Golden Gloves, but he was disqualified. He bit a guy.

He tried to bite his ear off.

He was a good baseball player, too, an outfielder in the St. Louis Cardinals' farm system. That's how he got his nickname "Bull." Chasing a fly ball he ran through a snow fence.

He lived like that. Flat out.

One night we were out drinking—myself, John, Manny Fernandez and Frank Emanuel, one of those nights. We left one party and we were driving along when we had to stop for a red light. John jumped out of the car, ran over to a fruit stand and grabbed a big watermelon. He ran back toward our car but suddenly he stopped and yelled: "What am I doing with this thing?"

He went over to another car and knocked on the window. When the lady rolled down the window, he dumped the watermelon on her lap.

That was just the beginning. We stopped at One South, a bar we liked to drink at, but it had been raining and there was a huge puddle outside. John and Frank Emanuel started chasing each other in the puddle. Manny Fernandez looked at them and shook his head.

"The hell with these crazy bastards," Manny said. "I'm going home."

I didn't blame him, but One South was close to the Villa Apartments so I figured I better stay to take care of these guys. That was a mistake right there. All of a sudden, John ran down a steep incline toward a canal in the park there. And he dove in. The problem was, I knew he couldn't swim too good. I'm not exactly a lifeguard but I dove in to get him. Now if I hadn't been drinking, I definitely never would've done it. The canal was slimy, like there were snakes in it. I hate snakes. But now I was in the canal and I had John by the shirt. Every few seconds the two of us went under, but then I'd pull him up again. All the time I was yelling: "Frank, Frank, help me get him out."

Frank splashed in, but instead of coming over to where I had John, he swam out to where the ducks were. He swam around with the ducks for a couple minutes. Finally he helped me get John out. We had mud and weeds all over us. Manny had taken the car so we decided to hitchhike home. When the other two wobbled over to the wrong side of the road. I'd had it. I left them and walked home.

But a couple hours later, I heard this big commotion outside. I knew John had to be home.

It turned out that after I left him, he had gotten into a big fight. He had lost his false teeth. And now he was really making a lot of noise. Somebody in the apartments had called the cops. When the cops came, one of them came up to his apartment to see what was going on.

"Take me to jail," John growled at him.

But in the next breath, he was John the nice guy. His voice dropped and he asked the cop, "You want a cup of coffee?" Then he got loud again.

"Take me to jail," he shouted.

The cop was looking at him, and I was trying to calm John down. The cop didn't know what the hell was going on. But that was just John.

He was incredible on a road trip.

He made a road trip an adventure.

Our rookie year, we were in San Diego, staying at the Stardust Hotel in Mission Valley there. Our first morning, me and Jim went down for breakfast and all the players in the coffee shop were passing the San Diego *Union* around. It had a big picture of a guy driving a golf cart along the Freeway there in Mission Valley. Above it was a big headline: "The Phantom Golf Cart Driver." The more I looked at that picture, the more it looked like John Bramlett in that golf cart. Sure as hell, it had been. After practice the day before, John wanted to move around town. But he didn't want to rent a car and he had trouble getting a cab. There was a golf course at the hotel, so he got into a golf cart and took off. His big mistake was leaving his Dolphin blazer somewhere, because the cops brought it back to the hotel to show George Wilson as evidence. But when George confronted him with the blazer, John said: "Coach, somebody stole that blazer from me right after we got off the plane yesterday."

On that same trip, a bunch of players were sitting by the swimming pool when a bellhop went by with a bucket of ice on a tray. Somehow the bellhop mentioned that the ice was for George Wilson, and when he did, one of the players leaped off his chair.

"Give me that ice," he growled.

He took the bucket of ice into his room, dumped a turd on the ice, tiptoed into the hall where George Wilson's room was, put the bucket outside the door, knocked, and ran. That night at the meeting, George Wilson was madder than hell.

"I don't know who shit in my ice bucket," George said, "but if I ever find out . . ."

Everybody broke up. I don't think George ever found out and we're not squealing.

The next week, we were in Buffalo for a game. About

ten o'clock Saturday night, me and Jim were in our room with my brother Joe, who had come over from Stow to see me. All of a sudden, out in the hall, we heard this awful racket. Somebody was kicking the elevator and yelling, and a woman was screaming. I opened the door and saw a middle-aged blonde hurrying down the hall with John right behind her.

"Who's that?" my brother said.

"That's John Bramlett," I said.

I hadn't finished saying it when the middle-aged chick came running back the other way, with Bramlett still chasing her. Bramlett tackled her, actually tackled her. Then he picked her up and flung her over his shoulder and started walking toward his room.

"If you're going to throw it around," he yelled, "I'm going to take it."

He was just trying to scare her. He succeeded. She pissed all over him. He dropped her on the floor and let her go. Later that same night, some socialites in tuxedos and evening gowns were having a party across the hall from us. All of a sudden, we heard somebody pounding on their door. When the door opened, John walked in—wearing only his boxer shorts, we found out later.

"If you people don't shut the fuck up," he yelled, "I'm going to come back and kill every one of you."

He turned around and walked out. Those people didn't say another word above a whisper. All we heard was them getting their coats and getting out of the room. They didn't want to take any chances on John coming back.

John had unbelievable balls. Unbelievable.

One night I was with him in Miami, and he was in a pissed-off mood. He mumbled something to this guy in a bar and the guy pulled a gun on him. John didn't back off an inch.

"You go ahead and shoot," John said. "But you better get me with the first shot because if you don't, I'll kill you."

It turned out the guy was a cop and that cooled it, but John was pissed off anyway. He was in one of his moods where he wanted to get in a fight.

He had a way of rubbing people the wrong way.

That same night, me and Bob Petrella, a safetyman, were with John and our wives, and John was still fuming. We walked into One South for a drink, but at the door three guys had given our wives a long look. When we got inside, John said: "Bob, take the girls over there. Jim, you stay with me."

I thought, Oh, oh, here it comes. No sooner did I open the door than John grabbed two of the guys and cracked their heads together. Then he whacked the other guy. The three of them got up and ran away.

Another time, I was riding home with John, Frank Emanuel, and Billy Neighbors from the airport after a road trip. John and Frank always grabbed whatever beer was left over on the plane to drink in the car on the way home. But this time there hadn't been any left over. John's wife Nancy was driving, and Frank mentioned: "I'd love to stop someplace for another drink."

Nancy glanced across at John in the front seat. She recognized that look in his eye.

"John Bramlett," she said, "don't you dare."

John sat there, not saying a word, not even looking at her. But at the next light, he bolted and took off down the street. Just as quick, Frank followed him. Nancy cranked that car and went after him, but he disappeared between some buildings. She knew enough not to bother to look too long. She drove me and Billy home.

He had a sense of humor, too. That season we had a bunch of guys hurt and the newspapers started playing it up. The next day, John came out to practice completely wrapped in tape, bandages, and gauze. He looked like a mummy. All you could see of him was his eyes.

John hung around with two other linebackers, Wahoo McDaniel and Bob Bruggers, but lucky for him, he wasn't out drinking with them in Denver the Friday night before the game there. Wahoo backed a car into a car that belonged to an off-duty policeman. Wahoo was a wild man. He's a professional wrestler now. Chief Wahoo, he's part Choctaw Indian. When he got a little wild with the cop, he got arrested. Bruggers was with him. At the station house, Bruggers phoned George Wilson for some bail money. George put up with a lot, but if you crossed him or made him look bad publicly, he'd really come down hard. Wahoo and Bruggers not only missed the curfew, they were in a police station. When George got there, he cut them on the spot.

At training camp, Bramlett, Wahoo, and Bruggers had been amazing. Between workouts, everybody else was too tired to do anything but take a nap. They'd play nine holes of golf. They were walking around in that hot Florida sun in August, playing golf like they were staying at a mountain resort.

They weren't around too long. Wahoo and Bruggers got into that jam in Denver, and after our rookie year John was traded to the Patriots in the deal for Nick Buoniconti.

I've heard that when John arrived at the Patriots' train-

ing camp the the next year, he roped off his locker and announced, "This is Bull Bramlett's area." I missed John but we got a helluva middle linebacker in Nick Buoniconti, even if he didn't seem to appreciate some of the stuff that went on at training camp. Like the time there was garbage all over Zonk's bed. Scraps of food, bottles, cans, beer and soda oozing into the sheets.

Somebody had played a trick on me, which was all right because I was always playing tricks like that on other guys, but I knew there was no way I could sleep in that bed. I rolled it down the hall and switched it with Billy Neighbors' bed. About an hour later, I strolled into Billy's room to see how he had reacted. Billy was sitting on his bed, smoking a cigar and looking across at his roommate, Nick Buoniconti, on the other bed.

"Nick," he was saying, "I can't imagine who did that to you."

Billy had switched beds with him. Billy had got to the room before Nick had, and instead of switching beds with somebody in another room, he switched with his own roommate. Nick was really pissed off. He was storming around the room, trying to clean up the mess. Billy just sat there, puffing on his cigar like W. C. Fields.

"I can't imagine who'd do that," Billy was saying. "I can't imagine."

We used to have some great towel fights. One time I was trapped in a room with John Richardson, a big defensive tackle from UCLA whose nickname was Shaky because whenever he got excited his body actually shook. He was a helluva guy, but in a game, if somebody did something to him, he'd get his wires crossed and his body would begin to shake. When that happened, everybody cleared out. The day of the towel fight, John and I knew a dozen guys were outside in the hall, armed with wet towels, but John had it figured out.

"Zonk," he whispered, "you jerk open the door and I'll throw a bunch of these towels."

But when I opened the door, Shaky never had a chance. He got hit with a dozen towels so hard he went backwards. Out in the hall, the other guys laughed and ran across the hall into Stan Mitchell's room. Behind me, Shaky's eyes got big and his body started to shake and he started to run in place. When he got mad, he ran in place. After he did his dance, he took off like a big-ass rocket across the hall, but just as he got there they closed the door. He literally ran right through the door. Crash, splinter. He ripped that door right off its frame.

"Shaky, Shaky," Stan Mitchell yelled. "Take it easy, Shaky, calm down."

Some of the other guys ran out through the shattered door. The others were trapped inside. They didn't know what the hell to do. Worse, they didn't know what the hell Shaky was going to do. Shaky was running around the room in little circles, like he was all three of The Three Stooges, but somehow Stan calmed him down.

Things like that went on at Boca Raton all the time.

Me and Jim Riley, a defensive end from Oklahoma, used to shoot each other with water guns, shaving cream, even fire extinguishers. Not sneaky, either. Face to face.

Jim Riley always was thinking of ways to burn guys. The biggest burn was with the girl in Cincinnati he raved about.

Our second year, about two weeks before we were to go to Cincinnati for an exhibition game, Riley dropped the word.

"This girl I know in Oklahoma," he said, "she's really something. She is really it. She's a stripper now in Cincinnati, and when we get there she wants to come over to the hotel and put on a show for the guys. She will put on some show."

Every few days, he mentioned it again. Just enough to keep everybody interested. Just enough to build you real slow.

The day we got there, some of the guys reminded him, "Now don't forget me, Riley, don't forget me." He winked and smiled. We had a short workout, like we always do the day before a game. As soon as Jim and I were back in our hotel room, the phone rang.

"She's here," Riley said. "Anytime you're ready."

I was dressed but Jim was jumping along, putting his shoes on. When we got to Riley's room, he and his roommate, Manny Fernandez, were sitting there, grinning.

"She's in the bathtub," Riley said. "It's a private show."

I opened the bathroom door real slow, went in, and closed it behind me. The shower curtain was across the tub, adding to the mystery. Except that when I yanked the shower curtain back, the bathtub was empty.

That goddamn Riley got me again, I thought, but I wasn't about to let on.

I pretended I was talking to her and I made some noises. I turned the shower on. I did everything I could to make Jim think there really was a chick in there. After a few minutes, I walked out.

"Man," I said, "that's the wildest chick I've ever seen."

By this time several guys had arrived in the room. John Richardson jumped up.

"I'm next," he said. "I'm next."

He hurried into the bathroom, but he didn't go along with it. He was out in two seconds.

"You goddamn guys," he grumbled. "I'll never believe you again, Riley."

I waited around because I knew other guys were on the way. Riley kept calling different rooms. Some of the guys didn't even wait for the elevator. We could hear them stampeding down the stairs. They'd haul-ass into the room, asking, "Where is she, where is she?" When it was their turn, some of them would say, "Heeere I come," and tiptoe in. Two seconds later, they were out. Some got pissed off but most of them laughed about it.

That was Jim Riley's best burn.

Riley was always doing things.

Our second year, when we were getting beat every week, Riley's defensive coach was Les Bingaman, a drinking, two-gun guy, just a helluva guy. He had been a 320-pound middle guard for the Detroit Lions when George Wilson was a coach there. Wilson put him on his Dolphin staff, then Shula kept him as a scout. Everybody loved him. When he died of a heart attack a few days before we beat the Colts in 1970, the team gave his widow Betty and his two-year-old Lester III the game ball. Everybody loved ol' Les, and he loved everybody. When he was the defensive line coach, Les always had a bottle with him on the plane coming back from a road game. Me and Riley had our beer, and with the shots Les was giving us, if we'd lost we never had any trouble forgetting about the loss.

Up at Buffalo once, we got the hell kicked out of us, 28–3, and we got back to Miami late that night. But there was no way me and Riley were going home.

I knew a nice little bar behind Fort Lauderdale in the cowboy community. It's next to a canal. Me and Riley went there and we were still drinking the next morning. But people kept coming over to console us.

"Too bad you lost," one guy said. "Don't worry about it."

"We don't want any of that shit," I said. "Leave us alone."

I meant it. We didn't want any sympathy. We just wanted to have a few drinks. Or a few more drinks. The more the people tried to console us, the more belligerent Riley got. The barmaid even came over and cooed at him. Then a big bullshit artist that I knew, a real bigmouth, came over.

"It doesn't matter that you lost," he said. "You're our team."

Riley's eyes flashed. I knew the bigmouth was in big trouble. Riley jumped up, grabbed him by the collar, and ran him out through a side door onto the dock by the canal. And he went right off the dock with him.

I sat there laughing. I mean, you had to see it to appreciate how funny it was.

I ran out on the dock. The bigmouth was in the water near the ladder now. I reached down and helped him up just so far, then I pushed him back in. But when I tried to push Riley back in, he grabbed me and pulled me with him. By now everybody in the bar was out on the dock. When me and Riley got out of the water, we started throwing the other people in. There must have been twenty people splashing around in the canal, yelling and screaming.

Riley came back into the bar, grabbed the barmaid, and threw her in.

Jim Riley even inspired me to do crazy things. One

time in Boston the night before a game, Riley and Manny Fernandez were in our room about half an hour before curfew. We were a few floors up in the Charter House hotel. Outside, some guy was honking his horn something awful. I opened the window and hollered at him. He got out of his car, hollered at me, got back in his car, and started honking his horn again.

"I'll fix this son of a bitch," I said.

I grabbed the Gouda cheese, the round yellow cheese in the red wrapper, off the room-service tray and threw it out the window at his car. It was the best pass I've ever thrown. It hit right in the middle of the guy's hood. Splat. Gouda cheese all over his car.

That guy came up and beat the hell out of Zonk.

The hell he did. He stopped honking his horn and he drove away. I think he realized he deserved it. That's what I mean about Jim Riley inspiring me.

Don't blame Riley. You threw the cheese, not him.

Jim Riley's out of football now. He hurt his knee in training camp a year ago and needed an operation. He had to retire. That's the trouble with football. Sooner or later some of your best friends either get cut or traded or retire. Like when we won the Super Bowl last season, I wished that all the guys we've known on the Dolphins could've been there to enjoy it with us. In their own way, they helped me and Jim and everybody else get there.

A guy like Bob Petrella, he got cut. He's still bitter about it. But me and Alice still see him and his wife, Cam, quite often.

I miss Bob DeMarco not being around. He's with the Browns now. He came to the Dolphins in 1970 from the

Steelers in a trade when we needed a center. He had been with the Cardinals for about ten years.

Helluva guy, from Rutherford, New Jersey, not far from me.

Bob DeMarco is a player's player. He'll always tell you exactly what he's thinking. When he was with the Cardinals, he spoke up about why the team wasn't winning, that there was a "communications gap" between the coach, Charley Winner, and the players. So they traded him. When he realized he wasn't going to start with us last season, he spoke up too.

Shula wanted to keep him as a backup center behind Jim Langer, but Bob felt he deserved to start.

It wasn't a personal thing between Langer and him; Bob's too much of a professional for that. He just wanted the Dolphins to guarantee his salary for the season if they were going to go with Langer instead of him. He told Shula either to guarantee his salary or he was leaving. He told him that early in training camp when he knew he had time to catch on with another team. DeMarco had guts, but he wasn't a wild man. When he thought he was being screwed, he didn't sit there and be nicey-nicey about it. He spoke up. More guys should do that.

He's lucky he did. He caught on with the Browns right away.

We didn't see him again until the day before our playoff game with the Browns last year. After our Saturday workout in the Orange Bowl, we were leaving just as the Browns were taking the field. I happened to have a team picture of the Dolphins with me, and when I saw Bob I waved the picture.

"This is our Christmas bonus," I told him.

He laughed. Then the next day, which was Christmas Eve, when we got to our locker room there was a Christmas present for us—a money clip with a dolphin on it for each player, a pin with a dolphin on it for his wife. I took my money clip, wrapped it up with a little note that said, "Bob, this really is our Christmas bonus," and sent it over with one of the equipment boys to him in the Browns' locker room.

Out on the field in the warm-up, we really laughed about that. I wasn't trying to psyche him. He's an offensive player, too. I didn't have to go head to head with him.

I just like the guy. I still like him just as much as I ever did, even though he's not on our team anymore. When he left us, I didn't suddenly hate him. Most fans seem to think that one team is here, another team is there, that the players don't know each other. They don't realize that football players get along great with each other. It's a very closed fraternity because there's so much respect involved. That respect is important. Like during the off-season I was at the Columbus Touchdown Club dinner in Ohio with Larry Brown of the Redskins. When a photographer saw us on the dais, he came over and asked me: "Would you do me a favor? Would you pose with Larry Brown pretending to be feeding you ice cream?"

"I'm sorry," I told him. "I'll be glad to pose with Larry Brown for you, but none of that shit."

To me, it would've made a hokey picture. Just because I happened to be on the team that defeated Larry Brown's team in the Super Bowl doesn't mean he has to feed me ice cream. He's too great a running back to be demeaned by a picture like that.

It's the pride of being a professional football player. It demands respect.

Most men, when they meet another man, they try to impress him one way or another. Maybe with their money or their clothes or their car or with a chick. But football players aren't that way because it isn't necessary. In the NFL, all the players really are your friends, not your rivals.

The guys on your own team just are closer friends, that's all.

10

Forty Different People

Our first training camp with Don Shula, he opened it with a 12-minute run. We were huffing and puffing through it when Paul Warfield shook his head.

"We didn't have to do this in Cleveland," he said.

He had joined us that year in a trade with the Browns for our first-round draft choice, which the Browns used to select Mike Phipps, their quarterback now. Even if Phipps develops into the All-Pro quarterback, it was one of the best trades any team ever made.

Paul Warfield is one of the all-time great wide receivers. He's also one of the all-time great guys.

He's tough, too. Most fans don't realize what a good blocker he is. As a wide receiver, he has to come across to throw a crackback block on a linebacker. He really delivers it. In the 1971 season he leveled Dick Butkus with one. Butkus called it one of the hardest shots he'd ever taken. But to be with Paul, he's not tough at all.

He doesn't like to argue. It's just not his style. He'll

give you his feelings on something, but if you start to argue with him, he won't continue. He's a very intelligent guy. And he's like satin. Not only in the way he runs pass patterns but in his whole personality. He's really a smooth person in everything he does.

He's very unemotional, very quiet. So when he does say something, it means a lot.

Like in our playoff game with the Browns last year. We had been the first NFL team to go 14 and 0 during a regular season. But we knew we had to keep winning through the Super Bowl or it wouldn't mean anything. In our first playoff we were losing to the Browns, 14–13, with about eight minutes left. Our only touchdown came when Charley Babb blocked a punt. We hadn't been behind in the fourth quarter since the third game of the season when we were losing to the Vikings, 14–6, in Minnesota, but won, 16–14. Now, against the Browns, we had the ball at our 20 after a kickoff. We were in our huddle, all our eyes flashing behind our facemasks.

"All right," Paul said quietly but firmly. "This is it. We've got to score now."

Then he went out and got the touchdown almost all by himself. He caught a pass from Earl Morrall that got us out to our 35. Two runs by Mercury Morris got us to the 45, then Paul made a leaping catch of another pass that got us down to the Browns' 20, a great catch. He leaped, juggled the ball, finally got a good grip on it, and fell hard underneath Ben Davis, who was covering him.

Paul just lay there. I knew he was hurt. I was just wishing he wasn't hurt bad. Luckily, he'd only had the wind knocked out of him.

Two plays later he ran a sideline pattern, and one of

the Browns' linebackers, Bill Andrews, shoved him. The interference penalty moved us to the 8, and on the next play the ol' Kiicker went in for the touchdown.

That's the way this team is. Paul got us going that time. Beating the Browns meant something special to him. He'd played for them and he lives in Cleveland in the off-season.

But in another situation, it could've been somebody else who got us going. In a crisis, I think everybody looks to each other to come through together. We don't have any special leaders. I think everybody in their own way is a leader. I mean on the field. When there's a team bitch about not enough tickets or something, the guys go to Nick Buoniconti, but that's different. Nick is a professional's professional. He's not one of the drinking, hell-raising types. He's very efficient. Hell, he's a lawyer.

Nick's really helped our football team. He gave our defensive unit the experienced man it needed.

In a game, Nick's in charge at middle linebacker, just like Bob Griese is in charge at quarterback.

Bob was in his second season with the Dolphins when me and Jim got here in 1968, but we're really only getting to know him now. Like knowing what to expect from him. Or how he's going to react in a situation. Or what he's thinking. Until now, I had no idea what was going through Bob's mind. He doesn't make friends easily or quickly. It's not that he's aloof. It's just that until he knows you, he doesn't open up. He keeps a no man's land between you and him.

He's changed a little. He goes out of his way more now to kid with a teammate.

I think that's because he's more secure. When the Dolphins were losing, he was chewed over so many times by the fans and the writers in Miami that he distrusted people. Now that he's more secure, now that everybody realizes and appreciates what a helluva quarterback he is, he's opened up more.

He's a different kind of person than me and Zonk, but he's a nice guy. Very organized. Very businesslike. In the huddle, he's not a yeller. But he doesn't have to be. He studies so much, you know that he knows what he's doing. You have confidence in him.

Sometimes before the huddle forms, some of the guys are clapping and saying "Let's go," and you'll see him looking over at the other team, just thinking about what play he's going to call. Doug Crusan or Norm Evans will ask him what he's thinking and he'll say: "I'm thinking about running that dive."

Then he'll go into a quick explanation of why. When the huddle forms, he'll call that play without any hesitation. That's important. I've been in huddles where the quarterback starts to call one play, then he switches to another. You know he doesn't have any confidence in the play, so you don't, either.

The confidence in Bob's voice gives everybody else confidence. There's no hesitation. No emotion, either. He knows what he's going to call and he calls it.

Bob sets the tone of our offense, the tempo of our emotions. When he's the quarterback and we score, there is very little jumping around and screaming. Because he never jumps and screams, and everybody else adapts to his tempo.

With him, it's a business. When we score, that's it. He turns and runs off the field, and that's it.

When he throws a pass for a touchdown, I'll turn to him and say, "Helluva pass, Grease." But all he does is wink or grin or say, "Thanks, Zonk," and that's it. He doesn't want a lot of applause. It's almost like he was embarrassed by it.

Earl Morrall is different. Last season, when Bob was hurt and Earl was the quarterback, he loved to let himself go after a touchdown. He jumped around and beat guys on the back. Even in practice he's more emotional. He's a very straight guy, set in his ways, the crew cut, the whole routine. But he's real. I appreciate that. One day in practice, he threw a pass that missed the receiver and he got mad at himself. He doesn't like to swear, so he jumped up and down and yelled: "Cheesy weezy!"

When the other guys heard that, they gave him all kinds of grief. They really harassed him. But he just grinned. He can take it. He'll actually say "dagnabit" or "horse manure."

Earl's different from Bob in another way, too. Like when the huddle hasn't formed, if somebody asks Earl what he's thinking, he'll say: "Nothing, nothing."

Even if he had a play in mind, Earl never would mention it until he actually called it in the huddle, like it was unlucky for him to mention it until he actually gave it to you. Earl can be emotional but he's not a rah-rah guy. We don't have many rah-rah guys. Norm Evans will come around the locker room before a game and shake hands with everybody, but he does it quietly, seriously. He says something to everybody but I honestly don't remember what he says to me. I'm not really listening. I've got my own thoughts. Anyway, what he says isn't as important as understanding what his gesture means—to have a good game, good luck, let's be serious. I always look him in the eye and shake hands with him, that's the important thing. Norm is like a chaplain. He wrote a book titled *On God's Squad*; he's very serious about religion.

Several guys on our team are religious. "God Squadders," we call them. Every team has a few.

We're not putting them down. It's just that being religious isn't our bag. We're different.

What they do off the field is their business, just like what me and Zonk do off the field is our business. I don't like to knock people who do things different than I do.

They're good football players, that's what's important. Norm Evans is as good an offensive tackle as there is.

Mike Kolen, another God Squadder, is one of the hardest-hitting linebackers around. His nickname is "Captain Crunch."

Tim Foley is a God Squadder and a good cornerback. He really works hard at his job. I like Tim, he speaks up. At a big meeting last season about tickets, Bob Griese had a plan based on the more years a player had in the NFL, the more tickets he was entitled to. Tim was opposed to that. He thought each player should have equal ticket rights, no matter how many years he'd been around. He was in his third year then, so he was fighting for himself. I appreciate that. But I thought back to when I was a rookie and we had John Bramlett and Ray Jacobs, guys like that. If a ticket situation had developed then, a young player never would have opened his mouth. If the ghosts of John Bramlett and Ray Jacobs had been in that meeting last season, Tim Foley wouldn't have known what hit him.

All the God Squadders just believe in a different life style than me and Zonk do, that's all.

On a pro football team, there are all kinds of different people. You've got forty players, forty-seven counting the taxi squad, and they break up into friendships between two or three guys. It's like with the black players. No matter how much integration there is, there always will be a difference between blacks and whites for the simple reason that one is black and the other is white. On the Dolphins, like on every team I've ever been on, the blacks drift together and the whites drift together because each has something in common, the color of their skin. But on the Dolphins, the important thing is that there are no racial factions. Nobody looks at each other as a black or a white. They look at each other as a teammate. That atmosphere has been dictated by two things. One, by winning. Two, by a coach who tries to treat his players equally. Sometimes he doesn't, but Don Shula always gives the impression of trying to do it. One time last season, I was walking with Shula toward our locker room when Charley Leigh's wife drove into the parking lot and waved at us. Shula didn't recognize her, so he nudged me.

"Whose wife is that?" he whispered.

I told him, and when we got up to where she had parked, he said: "Came to bring Charley's lunch, eh?"

He said it like he knew her all along, and she smiled. But that's Shula, and that's good, too. Some coaches wouldn't have noticed. Shula is thinking all the time. Charley Leigh is black but that's not why Shula did it. Charley is a running back who doesn't get to play much, and if I know Shula, he wanted to make Charley's wife feel that her husband was as important to the coach as anybody else on the team.

In the locker room, I told Charley about it and we had a good laugh. Charley's a quiet giggler. Charley's a helluva running back, too.

On this team, guys are always harassing each other about something. Like last season when Earl Morrall joined us, our equipment man, Dan Dowe, brought in an old maple rocker and put it in front of his locker. The rest of us sit on folding metal chairs, but Dan figured that since Earl was thirty-eight years old he needed something more comfortable. Earl really enjoyed that chair. But every so often, just to harass him, somebody would steal it.

"I'm going into the shower," Earl would announce. "That chair better be back here when I return."

It always was, too. Out of respect for the elderly. Earl is so old, he still has a crew cut. Bill Stanfill, one of our defensive ends, always harassed him about that.

"Your hair's getting a little long, Earl," he would say. "You better get it trimmed."

Bill Stanfill is one of the more quiet guys on the team. So is Vern Den Herder, the other defensive end. Vern really came a long way. When he was a rookie, I didn't think he'd make the club. But he lifted weights, he got bigger and heavier; he's really a helluva pass-rusher now. But he gets harassed about his name. He's always getting mail for Dennis Van Harder or Van Der Herder.

Bob Heinz is another quiet guy, and so is Jim Dunaway. They're defensive tackles. So is Wayne Moore, an offensive tackle. Curtis Johnson, our right cornerback, is quiet, too, but he's got a dry sense of humor. If you listen, he's really funny.

Marv Fleming is a helluva dude. When we played the Giants at Yankee Stadium last season, the dirt part of the baseball infield was muddy. Mercury Morris tried to cut in that mud, slipped and fell. Going back to the huddle with him, I said: "Merc, you're a dumb Hunky to try to cut in that stuff."

Alongside me, Marv looked like he wasn't quite sure what he had heard me say.

"What'd you call him?" he asked.

"A dumb Hunky," I said, like there was nothing worse than a dumb Hunky, a dumb Hungarian.

Marv really laughed about that.

Marv takes a lot of harassment about spending money. Actually, about not spending any money. But he's got a reason. When he was growing up out near Los Angeles, his father disappeared, leaving his mother and six sons. As the oldest, he's been the working head of the family ever since.

He's always thinking of how to make some money.

Like in the end zone at Buffalo last season.

He caught a pass for a touchdown and I was alongside him. I told him, "Helluva play, Marv," and as I put my hand on his shoulder, I happened to look down. Laying there on the grass in the end zone was a ten-dollar bill, a little bit wrinkled but spread out, just waiting for somebody to pick it up. I pointed at it and said, "Marv, look," and as I did he put one of his big shoes on it, reached down, and grabbed it.

"Don't I get half?" I asked him.

"No way, Zonk," he said. "No way."

That's the difference between me and Marv. I saw the ten-dollar bill and pointed at it. He grabbed it. He's a real money player, too. He's been on three Super Bowl winners, two with the Packers, one with us. When he's asked which team would win if those Packers played our Dolphins, he says: "Whichever one I'm on."

That's pride. That's what football is. That's what football players have to have if they're going to win. It's a cliché, but it's true. Marv was one of the first players Shula got, after he took over as coach. Marv had played out his option with the Packers and Shula got him in a trade for Jack Clancy, a wide receiver.

On our jet charters, Marv sits in the first-class section with Bob Griese, Larry Little, Nick Buoniconti, Paul Warfield, and me and Jim, and last season Earl Morrall sat in first class, too.

Our first two years, when George Wilson was the coach, all the players sat in the tourist section. But when Shula took over, he moved a few of us up front. It's an honor. But to me, the most important thing is that the seats are bigger.

Marv Fleming is a tight end but he's much more than a pass receiver. He's an even better blocker.

With our running game, that's important. He can block a linebacker. He takes great pride in that.

Of all the guys on our team, I think Larry Little has the most pride. He's the best guard in the NFL, but in 1967 he wasn't even drafted. He signed with the San Diego Chargers as a free agent. But he was ordered to report to training camp a week before the drafted rookies were to report.

"That really got to my pride," he once told me. "Hell, they were rookies just like me. Why should I be a week earlier than them?"

That's what I mean about Larry's pride. You can hurt his feelings easily. He's a very soft-spoken, easy-going guy. I make sure I really communicate with him as much as I can. He grew up in Miami, and when he was with the Chargers, one day I met him by chance in an auto-body shop in Miami during the off-season. At the time he was hardly playing with the Chargers but I had the feeling that this was one guy I was going to get to know.

Get the hat.

No bullshit. I really had that feeling. I even asked him if he'd like to play for the Dolphins so he could be home all year round. But he hemmed and hawed about that. I didn't blame him. The Chargers weren't doing bad then, and the Dolphins could hardly win a game. But he lived here. I told him: "I'll see if I can get the Dolphins to trade for you."

I was half kidding, but I did mention it to Joe Thomas, who told me that he already was working on a deal for Larry. We got him a few months later, and at training camp he told me: "You said you'd do it, Zonk, but I didn't believe you."

Get the hat, Zonk, you had nothing to do with the deal.

Maybe not, but I'm glad it went through. Anytime that Larry Little is out in front of me on a sweep, the cornerback coming up to try to make the tackle looks like he wished he were watching it on TV somewhere. When they see Larry coming, those cornerbacks have alarm in their eyes. Larry loves to chop them down.

But the essence of our team is that there isn't a white guy who's afraid to kid a black guy about being black. And there isn't a black guy who's afraid to kid a white guy about being white. That happens all the time.

Like before the Super Bowl game last season, there was a newspaper article about how the Redskins had put up on their bulletin board another newspaper article. In it, Lloyd Mumphord, who was going to start at left cornerback because Tim Foley had a shoulder separation, had been quoted as not being worried that Billy Kilmer would test him with a few passes.

"Lloyd," said Doug Crusan, "it says you're their 'Pinup Boy.' At least they capitalized the B in 'Boy.' "

Lloyd laughed. So did everybody else.

Another time one of our assistant coaches, Carl Taseff, was giving us a scouting report on a team.

"They've got a new boy at linebacker," Taseff said.

The new linebacker happened to be black. Hubie Ginn, one of our running backs, glanced over at me, grinned, then looked at Taseff and shook his head. Some of the other black players kidded Taseff about it later. Ever since, he's always made it a point to say "man" or "player," not "boy." The black players weren't uptight about it because they knew Taseff hadn't meant anything by it. Our team has never been split over a white player getting a job over a black player, or a black player getting a job over a white player. Shula comes on with the honesty thing so hard all the time, everybody accepts it.

"It's not who you are or what you look like," Shula keeps saying. "It's how you perform."

I've only had one bad situation with another player the whole time I've been on the Dolphins, and he happened to be black. Jimmy Hines was the other player. But it wasn't because he was black.

Jimmy Hines was a sprinter from Texas Southern who won the 100-meter dash in the 1968 Olympics at Mexico City.

But he couldn't adapt his speed to football. They tried to make a wide receiver out of him. But when he made a cut, he had to come to almost a complete stop to do it. After a couple seasons, he got cut.

He couldn't catch the ball. His nickname was "Ooops."

One time coming back on a plane, he got a little drunk. He was standing in the aisle, talking about how he was going to be the first black President of the United States.

"Hines," I said, "they could paint you green, and you still wouldn't be smart enough to be anybody's president of anything."

I don't believe he ever spoke to me after that. But him being black had nothing to do with what I told him. Hell, he could've been polka dot. It's like socializing with teammates. I just don't socialize with hardly anybody on the team except for Jim and once in a while with Manny Fernandez. First of all, I live up in Plantation, behind Fort Lauderdale, and not many guys live up that way. Second, I prefer to socialize mostly with people who aren't in football. I believe that when too many players are close off the field, they get to know too much about each other. It can make for a bad situation. They can start to get negative about each other.

Even worse is when the players' wives make a big society thing out of football. I really resent that. Coming from Stow, Ohio, I resent any kind of fancy society atmosphere. Because where I grew up, everybody was just everybody. There you kidded each other without ever being pointy about it.

When you get the wives together, social climbing is prevalent. Some wives are more concerned with social status than in simple friendship with other players' wives. I'm not saying all of them, but a small faction is always present. And women, I believe, because they can't punch each other in the nose, tend to be more acute in that kind of atmosphere than men are. Particularly men who are football players, simply because these men have a great deal of respect for each other. We're not afraid to knock the hell out of each other on the field. So we tend to respect each other's feelings off the field.

But the chicks aren't going to get into any knock-down, drag-out fight, so they pull petty stuff. Sooner or later your wife is going to come home and say, "Do you know what *she* said to me?" Now you've got trouble relating to your teammate because you know that the other wife went home bitching to her husband about your wife. Ballplayers can live together. But you put the families together, you've got yourself a problem.

It's not good for players to live too close together. I found that out my rookie year. Six of us lived either in the Villa Apartments or nearby over on Miami Beach—myself, John Bramlett, Billy Neighbors, Frank Emanuel, Dick Anderson, and Howard Twilley. We drove to practice at Miami Stadium every day in Dick's car. Afterwards, most of us liked to stop for a drink, but Dick didn't. He'd drop us off and then go home. But the trouble was, he'd get home in time for dinner and we wouldn't. When we finally did get home, our wives all had the same question as we walked in the door:

"How come Dick got home for dinner and you're just coming home now?"

Little things like that create friction. But the problem was that we lived so close together. All the wives knew what was going on.

Whenever Dick was late he was probably out hustling a business deal. He's always wheeling.

The way he's going, Dick Anderson probably will be a millionaire someday.

No probably to it. He won't give up until he is. I don't have much in common with Dick because I'm not that dedicated to business. But that's nothing against Dick. He's a helluvan athlete and a nice guy. He gets along great with the guys on the team.

He works as hard at football as he does at business.

He'll come up with a big play just when we need it. Like the AFC championship game against the Colts when he ran back an interception 62 yards for a touchdown, the one where he got six great blocks. That was one of the greatest plays I've ever seen. I can close my eyes and see all those blocks unfolding. But he knew how to follow those blocks. Against the Giants last season, we were leading, 20–13, in the last quarter, but we had to punt. Larry Seiple was hurt, so Dick was our punter. He got off a bad one, but it bounced off a Giant helmet and we recovered. Good or bad, he'll make a big play.

Dick's a conservative guy, whereas our other safety-man, Jake Scott, is a born gambler. He likes to take chances.

He likes to chase girls, too. Him and our other tight end, Jim Mandich, all they do is chase girls. But why the hell not, they're single. On a pro football team, there are all different kinds of guys. Some guys even take practice seriously, like Bob Matheson, one of our linebackers. Anytime that Shula hollers at him in practice, he goes crazy for the next five plays.

Bob clocked me once last season in practice. He doesn't do it on purpose. He just gets carried away.

We've got some freaky guys, too. Another linebacker, Doug Swift, is a new-movement type. In the front yard of his house, he put in a little nature-like pool with a plant growing out of a stone formation. He's got a big Weimaraner that he drapes over his shoulders and carries around. He likes music. He has a big pair of earphones with miles of cord tangled around everything in the house. He's a free-thinker.

Doug's our player representative, but Howard Twilley is always arguing with him about something.

Howard is a tough little guy. He's small and not that fast, but he's always a regular wide receiver.

Howard is not big on unions, any unions, including the NFL Players Association, and he's always threatening not to pay his dues. He always says what he thinks, which is good. And he's always complaining about something to Doug Swift, no matter what the subject is.

Whenever it looks like some issue is going to be a solid hundred percent vote, Howard's face changes. He's thinking that not everybody has given enough thought to it, so he'll disagree. Just to get an argument going. He's also concerned with governmental policy, with the big issues.

That's unusual in the locker room. Most guys are aware of what's going on in the world. But in the locker room, they fool around.

Me, Bob Kuechenberg, Jim Langer, and Larry Seiple have a standing battle of pulled ears, snapping each other with towels. Seiple is our punter, a very competitive guy. In the AFC championship game with the Pittsburgh Steelers last season, he set up a touchdown. Instead of punting, he ran 37 yards to their 12-yard line.

Shula always says that Seiple has the right to run instead of punt, as long as he makes a first down.

Kuech keeps me laughing with his stories about his dad who was a human cannonball in the circus. One day his dad was sick, so his uncle substituted. But his uncle's weight was different from his dad's. Nobody compensated for it in the powder charge. When his uncle got shot out of the cannon, he missed the net and hit the ferris wheel.

His uncle really got banged up, so Kuech became a guard instead of a human cannonball.

Kuech and Jim Langer, our center, always bring their lunches to practice on Thursday, to eat after the weekly weigh-in. Everybody starves down on Wednesday and Thursday morning to make their weight. Shula knows what he wants you to weigh for the game, so he sets the Thursday weight at about two pounds under it, figuring that by Sunday you'll have put on another two pounds anyway. So to make the Thursday weight, you've got to sacrifice. That's part of Shula's religious theme. You've got to sacrifice to win. Evidently it's working. Anyway, when Kuech and Jim bring their sandwiches in, I tell them: "Taxes, time for taxes. I'm a running back. I've got to tax my linemen."

I'll take a bite. They do the same thing to me, only they try to take the whole thing. I've got to wrestle them to get my sandwich back. But nobody ever gets mad about it. We're just fooling around. It's guys like this who make a championship team. Great guys. Quiet. Friendly. You can't hardly provoke them. But on the football field, they're as aggressive as hell.

11

Negotiations and Nixon

I wouldn't need a big salary to play this game if we just had to show up on Sundays for the games. It's the practices I have to get paid for.

I'd almost play the games for nothing. Almost.

Me and Jim enjoy the games. All players do. And we even enjoyed the first two weeks of training camp in 1971.

We enjoyed it because we weren't there.

We were holdouts. The two of us against the Dolphins' front office. Us and our representative, Ed Keating, of International Management, Inc., the Mark McCormack firm. The previous season, I had asked Paul Warfield about the McCormack firm. We lockered beside each other that year and I knew McCormack represented him.

"It's a good deal," Paul said. "He not only negotiates your contract and develops endorsements, he also handles your finances and income tax, and pays your bills."

That really appealed to me. I hate handling that stuff. But the big thing was that our contracts had expired. We wanted somebody to negotiate our new contracts for us. Me and Zonk wanted to stick together in the negotiations. We'd have more strength that way.

We wanted a real professional negotiator handling us.

Somebody who knew how to pound the desk for more money.

About that same time, Don Scott, a neighbor of mine and one of my best friends, phoned McCormack's office. He didn't know Mark but he knew of him because of Arnold Palmer's success. And he knew that Mark was expanding his firm to include football players. By now, Mark also has Dick Butkus, Jack Gregory, Ken Willard, Donny Anderson, Archie Manning, and Dan Abramowicz to go with Brooks Robinson, Frank Robinson, Pele, Rod Laver, Jean-Claude Killy, Jackie Stewart, Peter Revson, people like that. It turned out that Mark was as interested in us as we were in him. He assigned Ed Keating to handle us.

Ed was the perfect guy for us. He's in his mid-thirties, a regular guy. He likes to go out and have a few drinks. Best of all, he's from New Jersey originally, Atlantic City. He had to be a good guy.

I didn't hold the Jersey thing against him. We met with him in New York a few weeks before training camp was to open. Me and Jim told him that we each wanted the same money from the Dolphins and we were going to stick together to get it. We had heard that Paul Warfield and Bob Griese and Nick Buoniconti were up around $60,000. We thought we deserved to be up there, too. We figured two-on-one was stronger than one-on-one. And with Ed guiding us, it was really three-on-one.

But that day in New York, he tested us right away. Actually, he tested me.

"Jim," he said to me, "you're not worth as much as Larry is worth, are you?"

He was trying to split us, trying to pit us against each other, because he knew Joe Thomas of the Dolphins would try the same trick. But he didn't shake me. Me and Zonk were really prepared to stick together.

We knew we could do better together than separately.

Ed had taken us to the Palm restaurant. "Write down on your napkin," he said, "your top figure and your bottom figure for one year. I'll write down some figures, too, and I'll tell you what it'll be when it's all over." Me and Zonk each put down $75,000 as the top figure and $50,000 as the bottom figure. Maybe not exactly that, but within $1,000 of each figure. We hadn't really talked about it that much. When we showed Ed the numbers on our napkins, he couldn't believe we were thinking that closely on the figures.

Even so, Ed wasn't sure how long we'd hold out.

He was worried about Zonk surrendering to Shula.

He had read about me saying, "Shula reminds me of my father, they're both crazy Hungarians," and he thought I was close to Shula because of that, and that when things got tight I'd give in to Shula and go to training camp and Jim would be out all by himself.

Zonk straightened Ed out on that.

The shocker was that we didn't give the Dolphins any warning. They had assumed that me and Jim were going

| ALWAYS ON THE RUN

to report to training camp at Biscayne College in northwest Miami with the other veterans while Ed negotiated our contracts. Most players do that. But we didn't show. We were told later that when Shula got up to address the troops, he looked around and said: "Where are Kiick and Csonka?"

When the other players shrugged, Shula was so pissed off he could've bit nails in half.

Shula's meeting was at nine in the morning. At ten, the Dolphins' personnel director then, Joe Thomas, arrived at the Aztec Hotel on Miami Beach where Ed Keating was staying in a big suite. Me and Zonk were in the next room, listening.

I heard Ed tell him, "Well, your boys didn't report."

"What are you talking about," Thomas snapped. "They're over at camp right now. They were there for a meeting at nine o'clock."

"No, they weren't," Ed said. "They're not in camp."

Thomas couldn't believe it. But when he got to training camp, he realized Ed had been telling the truth.

A few days later, Shula arranged to phone us at my house. Jim was on another extension, so he was able to talk to both of us at the same time. He told us: "Every day you're out, it's a $200 fine."

"Coach," I told him, "we've got responsibilities to our families in this. We're not coming in until it's settled."

"We respect your opinion," I told him, "but we hope that you respect ours."

I had been in contract negotiations twice before, both times by myself. As a rookie, I couldn't ask for big money because I'd been only a fifth-round draft choice. I had signed with Pro Sports, Inc., a New York agency, but they didn't do much for me. I was naïve. I didn't know much about contracts and I thought they could really help me. But all they did was give me figures that I should ask for. They hardly talked to Joe Thomas, they just told me to be firm.

I had confidence I'd make the Dolphins but Alice wasn't sure. She talked me into asking for a two-year contract with a no-cut clause, meaning that even if I was cut as a player, I'd get paid for the two years.

Joe Thomas agreed to give me a no-cut contract, but it had to be at a lesser salary than I had asked for. To make everybody happy, I took the no-cut contract for $15,000 as a rookie, $17,000 my second season. I also got a $7,000 bonus. But going into my third season in 1970, I asked for $45,000, more than double my previous year's salary.

"Nobody ever gets their contract doubled," Joe Thomas told me.

"I had two good years, Joe," I argued. "Last year I feel I didn't get paid what I deserved. I want $45,000 this year."

"That's something you'll have to gradually build up to," he said.

"I don't feel I have to build up to it gradually," I said. "I want to be up there now."

"No chance," he said.

I knew I wasn't going to get $45,000, but I wanted him to know I wasn't going to come cheap. His first offer was $20,000 which was ridiculous, then he came up to $23,000, then $25,000. He kept on dickering all through training camp. After lunch, I always like a nap before the afternoon workout. But every couple days, he'd send a ball-boy over to tell me he had time to talk contract.

Jim bitched like hell about that. He wanted to take a nap but Joe Thomas kept sending people over to wake him up.

I'd go over to his office but I never stayed long. I never argued loudly with him but I let him know how I felt about my situation. Another factor was that after my rookie year I'd had Harvey Lakind, an attorney in New Jersey who represented some of the Yankee baseball players, prepare a letter to the Dolphins in hopes of renegotiating my original contract after the good rookie year I'd had.

Joe Thomas was shitty about that. His answer was "We can't judge salaries on performance alone."

What the hell else is there to judge salaries on? I sent him another letter, but he ignored it. I realized that the chance of renegotiating the second year of my original two-year contract was useless. So when that contract expired, I was determined to be tough in negotiating a new one. And when I reminded Joe Thomas of my letter he said: "Suppose you'd had a bad second year, we'd have had to pay you $17,000 so we took a risk, too."

"That's not the point, Joe," I said. "I didn't have a bad year. I had another damn good year."

I always found Joe to be a pretty decent guy except when he was negotiating the club's money. Then he was a prick. All he talked about was what I had done wrong the previous season instead of what I'd done well.

"I'm not going to argue," I told him. "You're going to tell me what I can't do, and I'm going to tell you what I can do."

I'd get up and go back to the room and go back to sleep. But finally, a few days before the first league game, he said: "I'll give you $32,000."

"You got a deal," I said.

Jim made more money than me that year. My rookie year, Alan Brickman, an attorney in Syracuse, handled my contract. He had handled a few other Syracuse players, like

John Mackey and Jim Nance, and he knew the ropes. Especially for a first-round draft choice. Right away, the Dolphins tried to separate me from Alan in the negotiations. I had a good offer from the Montreal Alouettes of the Canadian Football League that I was really considering, and that shook up Joe Thomas a little. One time I was in Alan's office when Joe called.

"Come down to Miami as our guest," he said. "We'll talk."

"My lawyer has to come with me," I said. "He's going to handle my contract. I'm not going to negotiate for myself."

"We're not going to pay his expenses," Joe said.

"I'm aware of what you're trying to do," I said. "If you want to pay for me to take a trip down there but not pay for my lawyer, fine, I'll pay his way down. I'll even come down without him. But that'll be your money wasted because I won't negotiate without him. If you want to pay for a vacation for me on Miami Beach, fine, I'll come down, but I won't do anything on my contract without my lawyer."

I went down, and I paid Alan's way down. The Dolphins put us in the Ivanhoe Hotel in Bal Harbour, on the beach.

Joe Thomas came over to talk, but he and Alan did all the talking. I even fell asleep once while they were talking. Eventually, they agreed on a three-year contract—$20,000 the first, $25,000 the second, $30,000 the third. I also got a $34,000 bonus, spread out over a few years and a $1,000 a month for five months of the off-season for working for the club in promotion and ticket sales. Part of the bonus developed when Alan told me: "I think I can get you a car."

"Good, I can use one," I said.

It was a yellow Pontiac station wagon, just what Pam and I needed with Doug still little. In negotiating with a rookie, a team uses a car like it was candy for a baby. If the rookie isn't happy, a car is always the big sweetener. In our fourth season, the Dolphins couldn't break down me and Jim with a car.

As the impasse continued, the only regret me and Jim had was that we missed the rookie show.

That was the all-time rookie show and we missed it.

But we heard about it later. At training camp that year, John Stofa was one of our quarterbacks. John is a fellow Hungarian, truly crazy, a real gypsy. John will do anything to get a laugh. This was Shula's second year, and a lot of guys were unstable in their position so they were really afraid of Shula, but John didn't give a damn. John decided that the rookie party the year before had been a bomb, so he went to a bar near Biscayne College and got this chick who had to be the all-time corner-bar sexpot. I mean, this chick would get up on the bar and take her clothes off and do gymnastic tricks, the whole thing. At the show, when all the rookies got through dancing in their jockstraps, Stofa came out.

"We've got a little surprise for everybody," he said.

The curtain opened and here she came, parading out in a little G-string. Some of the guys who had been half asleep were awake now, moving toward the stage for a better look. Shula sat there not moving, not too sure what to expect. All of a sudden, she flipped off her G-string.

Shula's eyes about popped out of his head. He didn't smile.

She put on some show, the all-time rookie show. And we missed it.

But me and Zonk were having a great time holding

out. Ed Keating had this big penthouse suite in the Aztec with the glass doors going out to the balcony overlooking the ocean, the velvet wallpaper, a nice little bar, the whole thing. One time Joe Thomas came over, and when he arrived, me and Zonk were sitting there in big stuffed chairs, the ice tinkling in our glasses. Just after Joe came in, there was a knock on the door.

"Here are your newspapers, Mr. Kiick and Mr. Csonka," a bellboy said. "I rushed them right up."

With all that service we had in that big suite, Joe Thomas realized that we weren't missing training camp. Little things like that drove him crazy. So did the newspapers because we had them on our side by then. The first day, Thomas had told Ed, "Let's not negotiate this in the newspapers." Keating agreed, but Thomas and Shula told the sportswriters that me and Jim didn't care about the other players, we just wanted ours.

That really pissed us off. That wasn't true. Joe Thomas knew it, Shula knew it, and the players knew it.

On the Dolphins, your contract and your outside interests are your own business. Nobody goes around bragging how much money they're making. The important thing on our team is that everybody is everybody else's friend in the locker room and on the field. I phoned Edwin Pope, the sports editor and columnist of the Miami Herald, and told him that our holdout didn't mean we didn't care about the other players. All it meant was that we wanted to get paid what we thought we deserved.

"You must be asking a lot," Edwin said.

"We're not being unreasonable," I told him. "What do you think they should pay us?"

"Maybe $60,000 each, maybe $70,000."

"Edwin," I said, "they're offering less than $40,000."

"Those cheap bastards," he said.

From then on, Edwin Pope was on our side. So were most of the sportswriters. The other players always had been on our side. How the players would take it had been a big concern to us, but Paul Warfield talked to Ed Keating every so often. Paul kept telling him that the players were rooting for us to get as much as we could. None of them seemed to resent that we weren't in camp like they were.

That time Joe Thomas came up to the suite, he kept telling us that he couldn't negotiate with the two of us, that he had to talk to us one at a time.

Ed Keating had enough confidence in us by then to agree to Joe's demand. We made a big joke out of it. Joe wanted to talk to Zonk alone, so I went into the next room. But when I came back into the room, Zonk told me everything that Joe had talked about. Right in front of him.

"You can't do that," Joe yelled.

"We told you we were going to stick together," I said. "We'll talk separately but we're sticking together."

"I'm leaving," Joe said.

I had been sitting there, trying to be civil, but I couldn't take any more bullshit. As soon as Joe threatened to leave, I said: "Good, get the hell out of here."

He really blew up then. He yelled, "You can't talk that way to me."

I apologized to him. But the negotiations were such a farce, I just couldn't stand it. Looking back, it was shitty of me to do that. I really felt bad about it later on. But at the time, it was a little funny. I mean, when I said it, Joe Thomas went pale and Ed Keating went pale and I thought, Oh shit, now I've done it.

I didn't go pale. I loved it. Zonk took the words right out of my mouth.

The next few days, negotiations broke down. But me and Jim had a helluva time.

One night we were in Fort Lauderdale at Bachelors III, the club Joe Namath owns. We were having a few drinks with Bobby Van, who managed the club, and I told him: "Bobby, when you talk to Joe next, tell him we want to be traded to the Jets."

The next night, Bobby told me that he had mentioned it to Joe on the phone and that Joe was going to tell Weeb Ewbank about it. Nothing ever came of it, but me and Zonk weren't kidding. We were disgusted at the way the Dolphins were handling our situation. Maybe that was the night we kept shuffling our cars. We had left my car at a hotel but we couldn't remember which one. We rented a car, but forgot where we left it. Then somebody let Zonk borrow their car so we could look around for the other one. We had a car that wasn't ours, we didn't know where the car was that we'd rented, and we didn't know where my car was.

That was the day Alice called up the Aztec, asking for Jim, but he was upstairs in the sauna bath.

"He's not here," Ed Keating said, "but he must be around here someplace. His hat's still here."

Alice was satisfied. Jim's hat was there, so Alice decided not to kill him for not being there.

Almost every day, we were down at Jim's house in south Miami for lunch. Me and Jim would jump in the pool, and little Brandon would be sitting by the edge of the pool and Alice would ask Jim what kind of a sandwich he wanted for lunch.

"Roast beef," he'd say.

"No roast beef. Ham."

Or if he wanted ham, all she had was roast beef. They'd argue for an hour, then Alice would go down to the store. In the afternoon, we'd go to a high school field and run half a mile. One time down near Jim's house, there must've been a couple hundred kids running with us. Literally a whole Pop Warner League of kids swarmed us.

Another time, up at Plantation High School near Zonk's house, another bunch of kids ran laps with us.

"You guys can't run very fast," they yelled at us. "C'mon, you've got to run faster than that."

They were ten years old and they were running out in front of us. They were flying. Well, when you're ten years old, you can run forever.

After we ran, we'd go have a few drinks and a steak.

Near the end of the second week, Joe Thomas came down with hepatitis. He'd had open-heart surgery a few months earlier, so the doctors really were worried. They put him in the hospital and Joe Robbie, the principal owner of the club, took over our negotiations. He's a nice man, but deep down he's a big businessman. It's impossible to have a real friendship relationship with him. Sooner or later, a player doesn't mean any more to him, when it really comes down to it, than an expensive Xerox machine does. When a player is outdated, that's it. But after Joe Robbie and Ed Keating got together, they were close to settling it. On a Sunday afternoon, Ed called.

"We're pretty close," Ed said. "Close enough so that you can go to training camp tomorrow."

"Hell, no," I said. "Hold us off, because if we go in

tomorrow, they'll want us to play in the first exhibition game on Saturday."

We went to camp Monday night, but we didn't actually sign our contracts until Friday night.

As soon as we got to camp, the other players wanted to hear all about it. Jim Riley, Manny Fernandez, Doug Crusan, Bob DeMarco, they were in our room for hours. As far as we could tell, none of the other players resented what we'd done. And we weren't in bad shape, either.

Not compared to the other guys.

In the two weeks we had been away, Shula had run down everybody else. We were fresh. We were moving faster than any of them. He was glad we were in good shape, because it showed we were concerned about reporting in shape. Then, on Friday night, we had a contract ceremony in Joe Thomas's hospital room. The newspapers estimated we each got about $60,000 a year for a three-year contract, a good estimate. When we left the hospital, Shula took me and Jim out for a few beers at the Lion's Share, a little place near training camp. We must've talked for a couple hours. He even paid for the beers.

He could afford it. The club got $5,600 in fines from us, $2,800 each—$200 a day for fourteen days.

Over the beers that night, Shula talked about hair length, about how it really was unimportant, about how it really didn't make that much difference in life.

The next day he told me to get a haircut.

Even with this season to go on our contracts, the Dolphins have gotten their money's worth out of us. But whenever I think back to the 1971 season, I'll remember one game: the playoff with the Chiefs in Kansas City that went into sudden-death overtime, the longest game in pro football history. It delayed Christmas dinners all over the country because most people wouldn't leave their TV sets.

I was so tired that when we won I didn't jump up. If somebody had hugged me, I would've fallen down.

Our guys were whooping and hollering in the locker room, one of the few times that's ever happened, but I couldn't. I had the dry heaves. I lost about fifteen pounds in that game, just from everybody beating hell out of each other. With the score 24–24, I thought sure we were going to lose when the Chiefs set up Jan Stenerud for a field goal from the 31 in the last minute.

I even told Zonk on the sideline, "It's all over." I didn't even watch Stenerud kick it. But when I saw Shula jump up and heard all the guys yell, I knew he'd missed. I looked at Zonk and said, "I guess it ain't over." It took another twenty-two minutes and forty seconds of overtime. Zonk made the big play for us.

I wish I could've run faster, but I was just so tired. It was the first time I'd ever played a game and a half.

We were on our 35 and Zonk followed Larry Little and Norm Evans upfield to the Chiefs' 36, field-goal range. I had faked a sweep on the play, but nobody was following me. I was out there all alone with an official. I just stopped and watched Zonk go.

"Well," the official said, "that should do it."

But we wanted to get closer if we could. I got two yards, then Zonk got four to the 30. On third down, I wanted to run the ball into the middle of the field, not lose any yardage, and not fumble. I knew that if I ever fumbled there, I'd be through. I didn't fumble, but I didn't get any yardage either.

Jim didn't have to. Garo Yepremian kicked it right through from the 37, a field goal I'll always remember.

Garo grew up playing soccer in Cyprus and England before coming to the United States in 1966. Some NFL players seem to resent foreign kickers because they're not really football players. Like when Garo was with the Lions, he had to put up with Alex Karras making fun of him.

"I theeenk I keeek a touchdown," Alex used to say.

But a specialist like Garo doesn't bother me. Garo does what he does well. Whether a field-goal kicker should affect the outcome of a game so often is something else. But that's not Garo's fault. He works as hard as anybody else, and he's as talented in his own way as anybody else. At practice, he's over on our other field, practicing kickoffs all by himself. It must get very boring.

It's more talent than hard work, I think, but Garo's got the talent and that's what it's all about. For a kicker, he relates very well to the other players. That's not easy, because a kicker doesn't fit in with the offense or the defense; a kicker is just there by himself.

Most kickers seem to be loners, but Garo isn't. He's outspoken. When he joined us he worked hard and he was confident. He psyched Karl Kremser out of the job. Kremser was our kicker in 1969 as a rookie. But when Garo arrived the next year, he had better range. He had better psychology, too. They were roommates, and after practice they'd be taking a nap when Garo would jump up and practice his kicking steps, maybe just to show he had more pep. He had Karl crazy.

Karl opened the season. But when Karl missed a couple short ones, Shula activated Garo. He's been our kicker ever since.

Garo's field goal in Kansas City got us into the AFC championship game that season for the first time. When we beat the Colts, 21–0, we were in the Super Bowl for the first time. But we lost to the Cowboys, 24–3. As soon as we got back into our locker room, Shula told us: "We have to dedicate ourselves to getting back to the Super Bowl next season and winning it."

Winning the Super Bowl was an obsession with him. He had been the coach of the Colts when they were upset by the Jets, 16–7, and now he was the first coach to lose the Super Bowl twice. He really had a monkey on his back. As soon as we reported to training camp last year, he mentioned the Super Bowl thing.

"Just winning x number of games won't redeem our Super Bowl loss," he told us. "We've got to win the Super Bowl itself."

Every few days he mentioned the Super Bowl, and when the season started he continued to mention it. It got to be the underlying spirit of the team. When we finished the regular season with 14 and 0, some people claimed we had an easy schedule. If they'd played it, like we had to, they might not have thought that. Especially the first few weeks. In our opening four games, we had to play three tough games on the road with teams that figured to have a shot at the Super Bowl, too—the Chiefs in Kansas City, the Vikings in Minnesota, and the Jets in New York with Joe Namath healthy.

Easy schedule, my ass. In the NFL, no schedule is easy. We just made it look easy.

When we beat the Colts for a 14 and 0 regular-season

record, Shula got the game ball. But he gave it to Monte Clark, the offensive line coach, because we set the NFL season rushing record.

"There's only one game ball I want," Shula told us. "I'm sure you know by now which one it is."

We knew all right, the game ball from a Super Bowl victory. Every time he'd gotten a game ball, he gave it away to somebody else because he was waiting for the Super Bowl game ball.

"Going 14 and 0 is great," he told us, "but it won't mean anything unless we make it 17 and 0."

In our first playoff game we had trouble with the Browns, but Paul Warfield got us going and we won, 20–14. Then we went into Pittsburgh, where the Steelers hadn't lost all season, and won the AFC championship. The best part of that game for me was when Shula let us run on fourth down instead of settling for a field goal. Each time we kept going for a touchdown. The first time, in the third quarter, we had fourth-and-1 on the Steelers' 4 and Jim got two yards. Two plays later, Jim scored to give us a 14–0 lead.

The next time, it was fourth-and-1 on their 5 and Zonk got two.

Two plays later, Jim scored again to give us a 21–0 lead. As it turned out, we won, 21–17, but the difference was going for those two first downs and going on to get two touchdowns. If we had settled for two field goals, we might've lost.

Psychologically, it was important. It's always a letdown when you're not allowed to go for it on fourth down and short yardage. It's the exact opposite when you're allowed to go for it.

Those two plays were reflective of our whole season. When it came down to it, Shula said "Go for it" because he believed we had the confidence to do it. When the coach believes, the players believe. That's important because the coach can't do it for them. Shula was standing over on the sideline. All he could do was watch. I love the excitement of going for it on fourth down. I know the fans love it, but I'm sure they don't enjoy it as much as the players do. When you make it, you really feel like you've done something. When you don't make it, you feel just awful. Like late in the fourth quarter, we had fourth-and-1 at their 9, but I didn't make it. We had to turn the ball over. But our defense came through. Our defense always came through.

Another reason we did so well in the second half against the Steelers was that Shula put Bob Griese in. Earl Morrall had saved us after Bob got hurt in the fifth game. But when Bob was able to play against the Browns, we thought Shula should've put him in. And we thought that Bob should've started the Steeler game. Bob is our quarterback, Bob is our true leader. He's a master at calling plays. Not that Earl isn't, but Bob is just great. The second half, he had the Steelers so confused they didn't know what they were doing. He's a master at hitting a defense at its weakest spot. So when Shula announced that Bob would start the Super Bowl, some fans wondered if it was a mistake. But in our minds, he should've started Bob earlier.

Bob's always in charge. In the Steeler game, some guys were babbling in the huddle one time, but Bob just said "Shut up" and everybody did.

We were in the Super Bowl game against the Redskins, but President Nixon came out for the Redskins, which was funny to us. The year before, when we played the Cowboys, he came out for us. He phoned Shula and even gave him a play that he thought would work—a pass to Warfield on a down-and-in pattern.

It didn't work. But that was our fault, not his.

When the President gets involved in the Super Bowl by coming out for one of the teams, he's just trying to show that he's interested in sports, like everybody else, even though he's got so many other things to worry about. To me, his interest isn't a plus or a minus. But as far his football knowledge is concerned, I think that's a big joke.

By his position, when the President advocates football, he's implying it's great. He makes it an apple-pie thing. The danger is that some people then think everything is right with football. They push little kids into organized football without realizing that when there's too much organization by grownups, it's the grownups' game, not the kids' game.

When the President came out for the Redskins, we didn't feel he had deserted us. We liked it that way.

In the locker room, I told some guys, "If he's rooting for the Redskins, I don't see how we can lose."

12

The Ring

Two weeks between the conference championship games and the Super Bowl is too long, too dragged out. One week is enough.

But if it was only one week, we wouldn't have any nights out without curfew. They're the best part of the Super Bowl week.

That's true. Like the Sunday we got to Los Angeles to play the Redskins, our jet charter landed in Long Beach, where we were staying in the Edgewater Hyatt House motel. But we were up in L.A. quick enough. We didn't have anything to do the next day except show up for picture day, so there was no curfew. We found a nice little place in Marina Del Rey, where we just drank and listened to music.

Jim has an uncanny sense for smelling out a bar. I mean, a specific bar. We were looking for The Basement in Marina Del Rey, but we went the wrong way down one of the freeways and had to get off, turn around and come back. We didn't know where we were going, but we were in the general area and that's all Jim needed. He happened onto it. He's got a real bar nose. He really can smell them.

It's what's in the bars that I smell.

Then on Monday, after picture day, we drove up to Beverly Hills and walked around shopping. On the way back, we got caught in rush-hour traffic, so we pulled off the freeway and stopped in a dumpy little bar.

That was the second bar.

By chance, some of the other Dolphins were there. Dick Anderson was playing the pinball machine, Jake Scott and Jim Mandich were drinking, so we played a little pinball and shot some pool. Then we went back to Marina Del Rey and had dinner in Charley Brown's, then we went over to The Basement again for a few drinks.

It was our last night out.

After that, we drove down to Newport Beach and drank some more. We were at the bar in some little place when I noticed Jim talking to a big guy. When the big guy left, I nudged Jim.

"Who was that?"

"Ray Schoenke."

Ray Schoenke is an offensive lineman for the Redskins, who were staying in Anaheim only a few miles away from us. But he was the only Redskin player we saw until Sunday afternoon. When the bars closed that night, we stopped in a couple massage parlors and looked around.

They were packed, so we left. Massage parlors are a thriving business there.

We got back to the motel around four, but we had to be up Tuesday at ten-thirty with a few other players for the Super Bowl press conference. We did it Wednesday and Thursday, too.

I had such a hangover. Tuesday was a very bad day for me.

Most of the questions were routine, but I had one that was different. One writer asked me, "In all of American history, what person do you admire the most?" I asked him for a day to think about it. My choice was Adlai Stevenson. When he ran for President in 1952 I was only five years old, but when he ran again in 1956 I was nine and he really impressed me with his complete confidence and his short-phrase humor. I've been around some football coaches who think they're orators, but Adlai Stevenson really was.

I had the same question every day. "How do you feel about Mercury Morris playing so much?"

I answered it as best I could at the time. I had to be diplomatic. I didn't want to start a big hassle with the Super Bowl coming up. But to me, the situation went back to when I didn't finish the 12-minute run Shula has at training camp. Right before camp, I had a bad case of flu. The day I reported, I hadn't worked out for a week. I'd also said something I shouldn't have.

"If I wanted to run," I said, "I would've gone out for cross-country in high school."

Shula didn't appreciate that one. After about 8 minutes of the run, I had to stop. My legs weren't tired. But my chest still was congested from the flu. I couldn't breathe. I stopped running and began to walk. Alongside me, Zonk stopped, too. Shula hurried over.

"Are you guys trying to defy me in front of the rest of the team?" he said. "This is a forty-man team."

It would've been a thirty-nine-man team if I'd kept running, because I would've dropped dead. Zonk didn't have to stop. He did it for me. Then, a few days later, I pulled a thigh muscle. When the exhibition games were about to start, Shula told me: "We want to get a good look at Merc."

"That's all right with me," I said.

It really was, because I don't like exhibition games. I don't know any veterans who do. As the games went on, my thigh got better but I still wasn't playing. I told Shula that I felt good, that I was in shape, but he said: "We want to give Merc an opportunity."

Merc had bitched about not playing against the Cowboys when we lost the Super Bowl game, and Shula was trying to be fair to him. But he wasn't being fair to me. The week before the first league game, the question started to be asked as to whether me or Merc would start. I thought the answer was obvious. After the four good years I'd had, I thought deep down that I had to start, that I should start. So when I read in the paper that Merc was going to start, I couldn't believe it. Not just that Merc was starting but that Shula had told the writers before he told me. That really pissed me off. But when the writers asked me about it, I tried to be cool.

"Who starts doesn't make any difference. I just want to play."

Except that in the opener at Kansas City, I hardly played. At least not until after the game had been decided. When you're a ballplayer, you want to play while the game is being decided, not after. I had another talk with Shula.

"Merc did a great job," he told me.

"I'm not knocking that," I said. "I think Merc's a

helluva ballplayer. I just want to know where I stand."

"It was just one of those things. Things were going well with Merc in there, so we kept him in. You played."

"Not when it counted."

Deep inside, he had to know that it didn't mean shit by the time I got into that game. As the season went on, I shared the job with Merc, which was a very difficult situation for me to accept as a ballplayer. The big thing for me wasn't not playing all the time, but the sudden bringdown of not playing all the time. My first four years, I went over 1,000 yards rushing and receiving each year. As it turned out last year, in our seventeen games, I lined up for more plays than Merc did, 551 to 535, according to Shula's charts. But he had more opportunities to run the ball, 231 to 171. Another thing, when I ran it, very often it was short-yardage situations, where if I got two or three yards for a first down, fine, but it was only two or three yards. I didn't run many sweeps. I didn't run many screen passes either. Those are the plays where a running back gets his big yardage.

Maybe this will prolong my career. But when you're a ballplayer, you can't accept that. The more I play, the better I play. It's hard for me to run the ball when I'm in and out. I felt like I was working for Western Union.

High school, college, four years of pro, I was playing all the time. All of a sudden, I wasn't playing all the time. Considering the situation, me and Merc got along very well. We're very good friends. That's one reason I didn't mouth off about the situation. I didn't want to bitch that I should've been playing all the time, even though deep inside I had to think that way. I didn't want to say it because if I did, it would sound like I was downgrading my teammate, like I thought Merc wasn't as good as everybody thought he was. Hell, that wouldn't have been fair to him.

As far as ability goes, I thought Merc should be playing

all the time. But as far as ability goes, I thought I should be playing all the time, too.

Merc handled the situation well, too. He knew I didn't like it, but he also knew I didn't hold it against him personally. He once was quoted:

"The opportunity at training camp was all I really wanted. People had been saying, 'If Jim gets hurt, you'll play more,' but I didn't want that situation. That's not a healthy situation for Jim or for me. To descend into this situation gradually, especially the way Jim and I are playing it, it's easier to do it this way than to not really know when you're going to be playing and suddenly have to play for a long time. People wonder about my relationship with Jim now, but I never think about it in those terms. The more I've played, and the more I've been involved with both Jim and Larry, the closer all three of us are now. There's no animosity by Jim, and there's none by me. Every time he comes off the field, we give five to each other, to acknowledge to do your thing now. I don't try to outdo him. I try to do my best. He tries to do his best. And that can only help the team."

It did help the team. Together, me and Merc were the NFL's best running back. Between us, in the seventeen games, we ran for more than 1,800 yards and scored twenty-two touchdowns.

Despite the situation, me and Merc get along very well. If anything, it brought us closer together instead of separating us. His wife, Dorothy, and Alice got to be good friends. One night the week before we went to L.A. for the Super Bowl, they talked for about two hours on the phone. I never resented Merc's success because it was the team's success, but I did resent that after four years, I wasn't playing all the time. Like if Merc ran for 20 yards, I got pissed

*off. But not at him. I got pissed off because goddamnit,
that should've been me running the ball.*

I resented it, too. Not because Merc wasn't a good
back, but because Jim was a good back for four years and
was a good back last year. Jim shouldn't have been subjected
to somebody taking his position. That's the one decision
Shula's made that he did out of spite. Because we didn't
run his goddamn 12 minutes for him at training camp.
That's why he did it. To get back at us. I'm sure of that. I
believe that. And it's not something that I'm saying behind
Shula's back. I told it to him when it happened. We talked
about it in his office.

Shula and I have a good relationship as far as being
able to talk with each other. I'm not afraid to tell him what
I think because goddamn it, that's what I think. If he can't
live with me not seeing his point of view simply because
he's got the power, then I wasn't cut out to play for him.
Just because he's got the power, I don't have to smile at
everything he does. When this situation with Jim and Merc
developed last season, I paid Shula the respect of not saying
controversial shit to him in front of other people.

But in his office, we had some deep discussions. I'm
sure he knows that I don't like everything he does. But he
doesn't hold it against me because I pay him the respect of
not trying to show him up. The way I saw it, Shula handed
Merc the opportunity at Jim's expense. Not only handed
Merc the opportunity but stepped on Jim's pride with no
qualms. Step on Shula's pride and see how he reacts. Football is pride. When you don't respect the other man's pride,
you're wrong.

The one thing I want to be very careful about is not
to make Mercury look like a bad guy in this. Mercury was

trying to get ahead, like anybody else. And he did it without being shitty, without trying to put bad words on Jim. That's an appreciated thing because this situation could've been a real shitty thing. Mercury was smart enough not to do that. He tried to put as much pressure on Shula as he could in order to get a shot. And he got it. I don't blame him for that. It just so happened that it was Jim's position.

It works the other way. I could've been shitty about it. Very easily. Really shitty.

But it wouldn't have accomplished anything. It just would've made it all the worse.

It would've accomplished a lot personally for me. If I had come out with something, it wouldn't have been against Mercury, it would've been against the way it happened. I would've complained that Shula screwed me. Mercury just did what he was supposed to do. Shula is the one who screwed me.

Just because we didn't run his goddamn 12 minutes.

Me and Merc have a good relationship, I want that clear. Like after I scored what was the winning touchdown in the playoff game with the Browns, he jumped up into my arms and hugged me when I got to the sideline. It wasn't an act. It was very genuine. He didn't have to do it. I like him. Before practice every day, we talk a lot. He's a sharp guy.

When he was a rookie in 1969, he was very boisterous, very pushy and cocky. I didn't like him a bit. Lots of guys didn't like him. Lots of coaches didn't like him, either. But the first year with Shula, he started changing. I don't know if it was Shula or just the fact that he matured a little bit. But he wasn't as cocky. Since then, he's done a complete change-about.

Merc's smarter than the average person. He's really quick. He likes the right wing and the razzle-dazzle talk. When he gets into that, I don't really listen to him. But when he settles down and really wants to communicate, he's sharp. He's intelligent and he's aware. He's very aware because he makes himself very aware, that's why I like him.

But as much as me and Merc talk, we never talk about our situation. He realizes I know, and I realize he knows. We don't have to talk about it. He knows that I think I should've played all the time, and I know that he thinks he should've played all the time. Because we each had pride in our own ability.

There's an insight right there as to why there was no problem between them. Both guys were aware as to how the other one felt, and both guys were sympathetic to the other's feelings. Therefore the situation never developed into a crisis between personalities that might've disrupted the team. The two guys themselves were above that shit.

As much as the writers asked me about my situation during Super Bowl week, I didn't consider the questions to be a hassle. It's part of the week.

I don't like Super Bowl week. Tickets. Hotel rooms. Especially tickets. People think players get tickets like they were confetti. Tickets aren't free for us. I get tired paying for somebody else's tickets. You have to pay for them first, then it's hard to ask people for the money because you know they assume you get them free. Some people offer to pay, but not many. Tickets burn me up.

It's a hassle. But then again, you've got to think, if you weren't in the Super Bowl you wouldn't have to do it. I'd rather be in it, looking for tickets or a hotel room, than be home not looking for them. That's the price of being in the Super Bowl game. It's like signing autographs. If people didn't care about you, you wouldn't have that hassle, either. The hassle is better than having people ignore you.

We'd been through the hassle the year before. We knew what it was like. For the Redskins, it was their first time.

I don't know if the hassles bothered the Redskins or not, but they didn't bother us. As the week went on, I could see our team developing its confidence. Not overconfidence. Just the right amount of confidence that we were going to win. We had very good practices on Wednesday and Thursday, offensive day and defensive day. Things were really sharp. You could tell just by the atmosphere that everybody was ready.

Everybody really cared.

There was no nonsense.

I didn't look around for any snakes to throw at Shula that week. But it seemed like he said less than usual at practice.

I wouldn't know. I don't pay attention.

Shula tried to look like he was relaxed.

But he kept reminding us not to say anything uncomplimentary about the Redskins to the writers. He didn't want any headlines that might get the Redskins pissed off. Coaches worry about that all the time. But if the Redskins were like me and Zonk, they didn't read the papers anyway.

*I guess some guys buy all the papers to see what's going on,
but we don't. We didn't even see ourselves on the TV
news. I didn't care about checking on sports that week
because the Super Bowl was the big sports event and I was
in it. I didn't have to read about it. That week, I wasn't
concerned how my New York teams, the Knicks and the
Rangers, were doing.*

Shula kept telling us that he was more relaxed than
the year before, but I think he was fighting it. I think he
was trying to make himself believe it.

From what we heard about George Allen, the Redskins' coach, our players thought he was a little weird. But
we really didn't care what Allen was doing. We wouldn't
be playing against Allen anyway. We wouldn't be playing
against the bookmakers, either.

The Redskins were a 3-point favorite, but I thought
that was ridiculous. I don't think there should be a favorite
in the Super Bowl.

I got the impression that Shula didn't like the way
Allen did things. Like when he told us how Allen had
indicated to the writers that he had been fined by the NFL
for not putting John Wilbur, one of his guards, on the
league's injury report before the Redskins played the Packers in the playoffs.

"It's not true," Shula told us. "He hasn't been fined
for that. He'll do anything to get his team up."

Shula was really perturbed at Allen over that. He didn't
like the way Allen used that as psychology.

On the reverse of the coin, Shula was using psychology
on us, too. He told us, "They'll be up, and we really have to
be up for them." He was turning Allen's psychology into

his psychology, but blaming it on Allen so we wouldn't blame him for it.

Allen's reputation for spying bothered Shula, too. At the Tuesday practice, he had the equipment boys looking in the trees behind the fence in the little stadium we were in.

One of them shook some poor guy out of a tree. He looked harmless to me. Coaches have a great sense of paranoia about spies. To me it's ridiculous. Coaches talk about the game plan like it was a big secret document. Our game plan for the Super Bowl was the same as it had been for every football game I've ever played. Go out there and try to run the ball, establish the running game. If that doesn't work, then throw a lot of passes. That's all offensive football is.

Then, on Friday, the players' wives on both teams arrived. Shula handled it better than Allen did.

Allen had come out and said, "I wish the wives weren't coming." Shula was more diplomatic. He told us that there weren't enough rooms in the motel where we were to accommodate all the wives. So the wives were booked into the Beverly Hilton Hotel on Wilshire Boulevard in L.A.

"I can't tell you not to visit your wives," Shula said. "But we have to keep in mind what we're here for. It's not a pleasure trip. It's a business trip."

He made all kinds of excuses, like it was a long trip or he was afraid we'd get stuck in traffic. He wasn't any crazier than Allen was about having the wives there, but he handled it better. The year before, in New Orleans, the wives had stayed at our motel. It was a circus the last couple days. This time, Shula made out like circumstances were responsible for stashing the wives in the Beverly Hilton, where the team was going to stay the night after the game anyway.

I don't know how many players drove up to see their wives, but me and Jim didn't.

After the curfew went in Tuesday night, me and Zonk took it easy. We'd get up, go to practice, come back, have dinner and a couple drinks, go back to the room and fall asleep watching TV.

Some players might have thoughts of the Super Bowl all that week, but I didn't. I thought about it a couple times every day, but only for a flash. I thought about winning and losing, the great feeling of winning and the great dejection of losing. Like if we lost, I pictured myself in the locker room, feeling so sick, so super depressed, thinking about what I could've done differently that might've won the game. Just thinking about losing is enough incentive for me to want to win.

I thought about the game Saturday night, but not much. I don't really get into the game until I get to the locker room the day of the game. I don't have to think about it all week. I know I can get up the day of the game. And as important as the Super Bowl is, to me it's really like another game. It's still football. There are no new rules. We had to get up early for our pre-game meal at eight-thirty, but I never eat anything. I just sat there drinking my orange juice.

"Now the first play," Shula said at the meeting after the meal, "will be our Counter 32 Straight with a fake to Larry coming across. Jim, you'll be running the ball."

I was really surprised. I was starting. What surprised me even more was that it was a running play and I was running it. If it had been a pass play and I was in there to block for Bob Griese, that wouldn't have surprised me. But here I was carrying the ball. I imagine it shocked Mercury, too. He couldn't have been happy about it, and I don't blame him. All the way up to the Coliseum on the bus, I still was surprised. It made it easier for me to get up for the game. Not that I still wasn't myself. When we got into the locker room, I took a nap.

I took a crap.

There's always a big hassle waiting to get your ankles taped, so while I waited I lay down on one of the trainer's tables and conked out. When he was ready, our trainer, Bob Lundy, woke me up. All around me, the guys were joking around, like they always do. Doug Crusan was spraying designs on his arms with one of Bob's spray cans.

"You're starting, eh?" Bob said.

"Yeah," I said, "but hell, this is the second most important game of my life."

"The second?"

"I got a big sandlot game in Lincoln Park next week. I'm the quarterback in that one. I can't get hurt today. I've got to be ready for that one."

"You silly bastard," Lundy said.

Not everybody was as relaxed as me and Zonk were. But that's the way we are. If we were really uptight, something would be wrong with us. Other guys are just the opposite. If they were really relaxed, something would be wrong with them. Everybody's different. The idea is to be yourself, like Shula says. Like after the warm-up when Shula called everybody together in the locker room.

He was so uptight, when he opened his mouth he farted.

I don't remember what he said. I don't pay attention.

Whatever he said, it was shorter than usual. He usually goes for three or four minutes. But this time it was a minute, maybe a minute and a half. His voice was creaking. But when we got out on the field, that's when I feel the pressure. I'm always nervous in the warm-up. For any game, not just the Super Bowl game. But when they played the National Anthem at the Super Bowl game, all I thought about was winning.

I don't think losing ever entered our minds. I mean, the whole team. Nobody was thinking, would we win? It was how we were going to win and what the score would be.

On the kickoff, Mercury ran it back to our 24, then me and Jim went on the field for the first play. Griese would fake a handoff to me as I went to my right, while Jim came across from behind me, took a handoff, and went up the middle. It was a good choice, because on the first play, especially in a Super Bowl game, there's always a lot of pursuit by the defense. They're all sky-high. They probably would go for the fake to me.

Not enough of them went for it. I only got two yards.

We had trouble moving the ball the first two times we had it. But the third time, we got inside their 30. On third down, I was on the ground blocking when I looked back and saw Griese throw a pass toward Howard Twilley in the far corner. Twilley was wide open, which made me feel good. Then, when I saw the ball's trajectory, it looked like it was going to be an overthrow. But I saw Twilley catch it and the official's hands go up. I felt great. But the first thing I did was look around for a flag.

I saw Twilley catch it but I didn't realize it was a touchdown. From where I was, I couldn't tell where the goal line was.

That's the trouble with being in the game. Half the

time, you don't know what the hell is going on. You really can't see much.

In the second quarter, I was on the sideline when Griese hit Warfield all alone for what looked like another touchdown.

I looked around for a flag then too, and I saw one. Marlin Briscoe, who was in for Twilley, had been called for illegal procedure. From what Marlin said, he didn't jump offside, he just moved his hand a little before the snap. The official had to call it, I guess, but I wasn't pissed off at Marlin, I was pissed off at the official for calling back a play that big. Shula took Marlin out right away, and Marlin never got back in. Shula doesn't like mistakes. But none of the players got on Marlin about it. Hell, it could've been one of us.

We didn't let it bother us, but I think the Redskins were bothered. They realized they couldn't stop us.

We scored the next time we got the ball, after Nick Buoniconti's interception. On that series, Griese was using me and Jim to run the ball like he'd never missed a game. Then on third down Jim Mandich made a diving catch for a first down near the goal line.

That's where I like to be.

Jim smells that end zone, just like he smells those bars. He's a touchdown runner.

But that was a tough 6 points.

Usually we bust through and go two or three yards into the end zone. But we caught all kinds of hell at the goal line. We got piled up. I was across the goal line up to my waist but Jim was below me. I couldn't tell if he was across or not. I knew Jim couldn't see.

I could hear the Redskins yelling "No, no, no," and our guys yelling "He's in, he's in!"

I heard a big roar but the crowd was for the Redskins, so for all I knew, the roar was because the Redskins stopped us. I had this sick feeling that we hadn't made it. I was trying to look around but there was a mess of humanity on top of us, our white uniforms, the Redskins' burgundy-and-gold uniforms, legs and arms all mixed up, jamming down on my helmet. Finally, through this little hole in the humanity, I saw an official standing with his hands up in air and I beat on Jim's helmet. It was the happiest moment I could ever remember in football.

At half time we were ahead 14–0 and everybody was confident. Especially the offense because we knew we could move the ball.

On the Dolphins, it's not self-confidence as much as it is confidence in the other guys, both on offense and defense. We just know that if things get bad, somebody will make a big play. We've got so many game-breakers that sooner or later one of them will get his hands on the ball.

Like in the third quarter when Zonk went 49 yards.

That was one of the longest runs I've ever had, but the only thing I really remember about it is that Pat Fisher was running along on my right side, but he didn't really want to jump in front of me.

I don't blame him. He's the smallest cornerback in the NFL at 5-9 and 170.

He had to be thinking that his linebackers were coming like hell behind me, that they had the angle on me. Fisher had to be thinking that if he jumped on my back, Jack

Pardee and Chris Hanburger and all those other guys were going to knock hell out of him, too. He was looking to cross-body me at the knees, so that Pardee and the rest would stampede by him and land on me. Instead of letting him do that, I cut back toward him and hit him with a forearm. That surprised him. He didn't think I was going to go for him. It threw him off stride. But about four steps later, the whole crowd hit me. But they hit Fisher too. He got just as much a beating out of it as I did. That pleased me.

We thought we were going to get another touchdown, but Griese threw an interception in the end zone.

We had really rammed the ball down their throat on that drive. I didn't feel good about the interception, but I was confident the defense would take the ball away from them again. That's exactly what happened. Jake Scott came up with an interception in the end zone. His second interception.

Jake ran it out to midfield. But right after that was when Garo had a field-goal try blocked. Then he tried to throw a pass.

I block on field goals. I heard the ball kicked, but I didn't hear it get blocked. I didn't realize what was happening until I saw all the movement to my right. Garo had the ball. When I realized he was going to try to throw it, I couldn't believe it. Somehow he saw my jersey. He was trying to throw it to me. But the ball slipped in his hand. Mike Bass intercepted and ran for a touchdown. All of a sudden, we were ahead by only 14–7 with about two minutes left.

You never saw anybody as sad as Garo when he came

to the sideline. He knew he had put the game in jeopardy. We expected the Redskins to use an onside kick.

In the same situation, I'm sure we would've. What the hell, go for the ball. But they didn't. They used a regular kickoff, like they still weren't confident. They were hoping we'd make a mistake. They were hoping we'd give the game to them, instead of taking it away from us. They didn't know us.

On second-and-7 down near our 20, Griese hit Warfield at the sideline for a first down around the 30. That might've been the biggest play of the game. It let us kill a lot of time.

Larry Seiple made a big play, too. On fourth down, he had to get his punt away under a big rush. With more than a minute to play, we couldn't afford to have it blocked. He got a good snap from Howard Kindig and he got it away. Some fans take punters for granted but they shouldn't. Siep's the kind of guy to have in that situation. He's tough. He loses at cards, but he wins in football games.

After that, the defense swallowed Bill Kilmer when he passed. On fourth down, Bill Stanfill and Vern Den Herder almost made him disappear. When the gun went off, I was glad it was over, glad that we won, glad that we were the best team in football.

I was relieved. I was dead tired, more tired than I've ever been outside of the Kansas City overtime game. But it felt so good to be able to relax and know that it was the off-season, to know that the Super Bowl had been the last jeopardy of a perfect season, to know that now it was something we had, to know that now it was no longer possible for anybody to mar it. We had put together a perfect season. Seventeen and 0. Perfect. Even the coach was happy.

In the locker room, Bob Griese stood up to award the game ball like he always does.

"We had a lot of guys who had good games," he said. "Manny, Jake. Zonk had a big game."

Shula was standing alongside him, but Bob was pretending to ignore him. Finally he grinned and tapped Shula on the shoulder with the ball. At last Shula had the game ball that he wanted so bad. I don't think I ever saw him so pleased.

We were all just so glad we'd won. Maybe some guys thought about the $15,000 right away, but I didn't.

Neither did I, because I never worry about not having money. I don't think I could ever get ulcers over money. Some guys talk about the money jokingly, but they're always aware of the money. Maybe some guys were aware of the car that Sport Magazine gives at the Super Bowl, but I didn't think about it until somebody mentioned it that night when we were having a few drinks at the Beverly Hilton in Ed Keating's suite.

"Jake Scott won the car," somebody said.

Before you get into the playoffs or in the Super Bowl, you think, Gee, a car, isn't that great. But when it happened, it was an anticlimax. For me, 17 and 0 was the important thing, even if I'd got the car. I personally think Manny Fernandez should've gotten the car, but I'm happy Jake got it. That's the kind of a team we've got. As long as somebody on our team won it, Manny couldn't care. There's just not that kind of jealousy on our team. I think it'll stay that way. That's the nature of the guys.

If somebody on the Redskins had won the car, Manny would've been pissed off. But he didn't care about Jake getting the car, just like Jake wouldn't have cared if Manny had got it. To us, the important thing about winning the Super Bowl is the ring.

We each got a ring the year before as AFC champions, silver with a diamond in a blue stone. But whenever anybody noticed it and asked to look at it, they'd say, "It's too bad you didn't get the Super Bowl ring." That can really get to you after you hear it a few hundred times.

Especially when we felt the same way. Hell, the $15,000 won't last that long. You spend money. But you keep a ring.

It's a beauty, gold with a big diamond representing the Super Bowl, encircled by sixteen smaller diamonds. I'm sure it'll be the first piece of jewelry that I'll wear the rest of my life. There's a lot of pride and a lot of emotion related to it. I'm sure that when I die, my boys will want the ring.

It's beautiful.

It's meaningful.

With this ring, anytime you're having a drink and lift the glass, this ring really flashes.

Get the hat.

LARRY CSONKA

Miami Dolphins	Rushing			Pass-receiving			Score or Record
	att.	yds.	TD	rec.	yds.	TD	
1972							
Super Bowl VII	15	112	0	1	−1	0	14- 7 Wash.
AFC championship	24	68	0	1	9	1	21-17 Pitt.
AFC playoff	12	32	0	0	0	0	20-14 Clev.
Regular season	213	1,117	6	5	48	0	14- 0
1971							
Super Bowl VI	9	40	0	2	19	0	3-24 Dall.
AFC championship	15	63	1	0	0	0	21- 0 Balt.
AFC playoff	24	86	1	0	0	0	27-24 K.C.
Regular season	195	1,051	7	13	113	1	10- 3-1
1970							
AFC playoff	10	23	0	0	0	0	14-21 Oak.
Regular season	193	874	6	11	94	0	10- 4
1969							
Regular season	131	566	2	21	183	1	3-10-1
1968							
Regular season	138	540	6	11	118	1	5- 8-1
Regular season totals	870	4,148	27	61	556	3	42-25-3

Pro Bowl, 1970, 1971, 1972.

Syracuse University							
1967							
Regular season	251	1,127	10	11	125	0	8- 2
1966							
Gator Bowl	18	114	1	0	0	0	12-18 Tenn.
Regular season	197	1,012	7	7	48	0	8- 2
1965							
Regular season	136	795	5	2	13	0	7- 3
Regular season totals	594	2,934	22	20	186	0	23- 7

East-West Shrine Game, Hula Bowl, Coaches All-America Game, College All-Star Game.

JIM KIICK

Miami Dolphins	RUSHING att.	yds.	TD	PASS-RECEIVING rec.	yds.	TD	Score or Record
1972							
Super Bowl VII	12	38	1	2	6	0	14- 7 Wash.
AFC championship	8	15	2	0	0	0	21-17 Pitt.
AFC playoff	14	50	1	1	5	0	20-14 Clev.
Regular season	137	521	5	21	147	1	14- 0
1971							
Super Bowl VI	7	40	0	3	21	0	3-24 Dall.
AFC championship	18	66	0	0	0	0	21- 0 Balt.
AFC playoff	15	56	1	3	24	0	27-24 K.C.
Regular season	162	738	3	40	338	0	10- 3-1
1970							
AFC playoff	14	64	0	4	34	0	14-21 Oak.
Regular season	191	658	6	42	497	0	10- 4
1969							
Regular season	180	575	9	29	443	1	3-10-1
1968							
Regular season	165	621	4	44	422	0	5- 8-1
Regular season totals	835	3,113	27	176	1,847	2	42-25-3

AFL All-Star Game, 1968, 1969.

Wyoming University

	att.	yds.	TD	rec.	yds.	TD	
1967							
Sugar Bowl	19	75	1	5	48	0	13-20 L.S.U.
Regular season	155	583	3	17	202	2	10- 0
1966							
Sun Bowl	25	135	2	4	42	0	28-20 Fla.St.
Regular season	145	597	4	21	179	1	9- 1
1965							
Regular season	131	534	3	14	180	2	6- 4
Regular season totals	431	1,714	10	52	561	5	25- 5

Senior Bowl, College All-Star Game.

About the Writer

DAVE ANDERSON is a columnist for *The New York Times*. He has written eight books, including *Countdown to Super Bowl* and *Sugar Ray*, as well as nearly 200 magazine articles. He lives in Tenafly, New Jersey, with his wife Maureen and four children—Stephen, Mark, Mary Jo, and Jean Marie.